DAVID CROCKETT

THE AMERICAN HEROES SERIES

Amelia Earhart: The Sky's No Limit by Lori Van Pelt
Chief Joseph: Guardian of the People by Candy Moulton
John Muir: Magnificent Tramp by Rod Miller
Mary Edwards Walker: Above and Beyond by Dale L. Walker
David Crockett: Hero of the Common Man by William Groneman III
George Washington: First in War, First in Peace by James A. Crutchfield

Dale L. Walker, General Editor

DAVID CROCKETT

Hero of the Common Man

WILLIAM GRONEMAN III

A Tom Doherty Associates Book
New York

A Forge Book
Published by Tom Doherty Associates, LLC
175 Fifth Avenue
New York, NY 10010

www.tor.com

Forge® is a registered trademark of
Tom Doherty Associates, LLC.

ISBN 0-765-31067-8
EAN 978-0-765-31067-5

First Edition: November 2005

PRINTED IN THE UNITED STATES OF AMERICA

0 9 8 7 6 5 4 3 2 1

For my grandson
Joseph William Groneman

Contents

Contents

Foreword

The life of David Crockett, the prototypical "legend in his own lifetime," is a practical lesson on why the first duty of the historical writer—to separate truth from fiction—can never be entirely successful. His life has been so emboldened, by himself and those who later recorded it with "color" added, that black-and-white facts have faded to gray or disappeared altogether in the 170 years since he died.

Crockett himself was responsible for much of this dilemma. As a junior congressman from Tennessee he built, somewhat assiduously, a reputation as a babe from the woods, a "wag of the canebrakes," a close friend of what he called "ardent spirits," a lackadaisical backwoods "character" living by a simple motto, "Be always sure you're right—then go ahead!" His life, as he fashioned it, was a convincing and enduring mixture of tall tale and half-truth leavened by the occasional fact.

Even the French writer-politician Alexis de Tocqueville, a shrewd observer, could not peer beneath the superficialities. He saw Crockett in Washington in 1831 and was horrified that such a specimen could have risen to so high a station as the halls of Congress. "Two years ago," the Frenchman wrote, "the inhabitants of the district of which Memphis is the capital sent to the House of Representatives an individual named David Crockett, who has no education, can read with difficulty, has no property, no fixed residence, but passes his life hunting, selling his game to live, and dwelling continuously in the woods."

That truths are elusive and myth and folklore tenacious (something Napoléon knew intimately when he made his cynical remark that "History is fraud agreed upon") is nowhere better depicted than in the images that come to mind when we consider the place and manner of Crockett's death.

Three of these Crockett-at-the-Alamo images, scattered fairly evenly over the past century, illustrate the fact that the armor of myth around the Tennessean is so thick that few writers in the past 170 years have been able to do more than scratch it.

Probably the best-known picture of the Tennessean is the 1903 painting by Robert Jenkins Onderdonk, a Maryland-born artist who arrived in Texas in 1889. The Onderdonk oil, printed countless times on book jackets, posters, and calendars, depicts Crockett dressed in fringed buckskins, red neckerchief, and coonskin cap, a big hunting knife riding at his belt. He is captured in the colorful oil swinging his flintlock over his head to club the Mexicans advancing through a hanging cloud of gun smoke and over the bodies of the dead and dying behind the south-wall gate of the Alamo. The painting of this fatal moment derived from the artist's research in books on the battle and from eyewitness accounts, and was as accurate as the data available in 1903.

Another of these images, perhaps the most indelible of them all, appeared fifty years after Onderdonk, in the Walt Disney Productions miniseries *Davy Crockett, King of the Wild Frontier*. In those three hours of television, appearing in late 1954 and early 1955, the series theme song told of Davy's birth on a mountaintop in Tennessee, of his being raised in the woods so he knew every tree, and killing a "b'ar" when he was only three. More significantly, viewers learned that Onderdonk had it right: just before the fade-out of the last scene in the series, Davy (played by Texan Fess Parker) is seen swinging his long rifle in the midst of an overwhelming force of Mexican soldiers.

This classic rendering of Crockett's death also influenced John Wayne's Alamo movie of 1960 but was given an updated twist in the 2004 portrayal of Davy by actor Billy Bob Thornton in *The Alamo*. This 137-minute, $140 million film, unlike the Wayne hagiography, approached some truths about Crockett and the Alamo without being overwhelmed by them. Thornton's Crockett is a self-effacing, straight-talking man, embarrassed over the fuss made over him at San Antonio de Béxar, dismayed over being "penned up," and seeing the futility of defending the Alamo when hope for reinforcements dims. He cheers the defenders, plays "Listen to the Mockingbird" on his fiddle before the siege begins, and when the Mexicans breach the walls of the fort, fights with the same ferocity he displayed against the Creek Indians in Andy Jackson's campaign in Alabama, and in the Onderdonk painting.

At the end of the film, however, there is a serious departure from tradition. Davy does not die swinging his rifle against the foe; he is taken prisoner, brought before Santa Anna, and after he offers a bit of low-key but defiant taunting, is executed by sword and bayonet. This denouement, Hollywood's striving toward the dream to be more "historically accurate," derived from a memoir published in English 139 years after the Alamo battle. (This document, called the "De la Peña diary" after the Mexican officer who allegedly wrote it, has long been suspect, a subject of controversy, and is treated in detail in this book.)

These few examples of the images handed down to us, out of hundreds that could be cited, illustrate the problem of separating the Crockett legend from the real man and his life.

William Groneman knows about heroes.

He recently retired from the New York City Fire Department with the rank of captain after a twenty-four-year career. He served as commander of Engine Company 308 and worked at Ground Zero just hours after the attack on the World Trade Center on September 11, 2001. And, he is a world authority on the Alamo and the lives and deaths of those who fought the battles of the Texas revolution. After decades of research and such published works as *Eyewitness to the Alamo, Death of a Legend— The Myth and Mystery Surrounding the Death of Davy Crockett, Battlefields of Texas,* and *Alamo Defenders,* he was determined, in writing this book, to "show the Crockett beneath the myth."

"He had a good mind, a knack of learning from experience and the experiences of others he befriended," the author says. "He had an understated, homespun humor; was a tireless worker of great strength; a woodsman, marksman, hunter— like his fellow Tennessean, Alvin "Sergeant" York, the World War One hero. Like York, Crockett was a courageous soldier and a man who wanted to improve the lot of his people.

"I have concentrated on him as such a man and not the grotesque figure of the Crockett almanacs, or the folklore caricatures, or the Hollywood renditions. The real David Crockett was infinitely more interesting than his self-made legends or those fabricated after he died."

As to his death at the Alamo, Groneman reminds us that Crockett was "always searching for more 'elbow room' and Texas offered plenty of it." What is important, he says, "is that he sought a new life in Texas and joined the defenders of the Alamo, willing to fight for what he sought. He didn't have to be there. He had opportunities to leave and return to Tennessee, but he was a man of honor and stayed, and died a hero."

—Dale L. Walker

DAVID CROCKETT

Introduction

Early in the day of March 6, 1836, Generalissimo Antonio López de Santa Anna inspected the smoking ruins of the former mission San Antonio de Valero, known as the Alamo, just outside the town of San Antonio de Béxar, Texas. As the absolute ruler of Mexico, Santa Anna personally commanded the army that had taken the Alamo by storm that morning.

When he entered the fort to inspect the scene he insisted that his policy of no quarter for foreign invaders be carried out, ordering the immediate executions of a number of Alamo defenders who had managed to survive the battle. Following these executions, Santa Anna asked that the bodies of the rebel leaders be pointed out to him. He saw the corpses of William Barret Travis, a young firebrand who had helped foment this revolt, and James Bowie, an ambitious adventurer who had married into a prominent Mexican family of Texas. In addition to these, the acknowledged commanders of the Alamo, he asked to be shown the body of one other man.

Unlike Travis and Bowie, who had lived in Texas for years, the object of the Mexican commander's curiosity had entered the territory only two months earlier, and had been in the town of San Antonio less than a month. Santa Anna only could have become aware of this American's presence in the garrison through information from citizens of San Antonio who had come to know the American in the days prior to the siege. As he looked on the battered and bloody form of this forty-nine-year-old frontiersman, it is unlikely that the general knew that he stood above the remains of one of the most beloved and celebrated men in the United States. In a victory message to his government written later in the day, he mentioned the man by name, but attached no particular significance to him.

To Santa Anna the dead man had been nothing more than a pirate, as he considered all the men of the Alamo's garrison. He would not have known, nor would he have cared, that the man had been a husband and father, a Tennessean, born into poverty, who as a child began working at jobs that demanded of him strength and responsibility beyond his years.

The broken body would not have revealed how tough the living man had been, or how he had survived incredible near-fatal incidents throughout his life. The general had never heard the stories of the man who waded chest-deep through icy rivers, barely survived a riverboat wreck by being dragged by his arms through a porthole, or who descended into a crevice armed only with a knife to finish off a wounded bear. He could not have known that this man had served honorably in the United States' Creek Indian war in 1813 as a sergeant of volunteers. Nor would he have understood the contradictions of the man who later supported the rights of Southeastern Indian tribes not to be moved from their ancestral lands by the United States government.

Santa Anna was unaware that the dead man had spent a good portion of his life in public service as a local magistrate, militia officer, state legislator, and United States congressman. It would have bewildered the dictator to know that this person had achieved this position despite the fact that he was a natural rebel who refused to follow the demands of any political party, who openly opposed the president of the United States, and made enemies of two future presidents.

As an opportunist who had once switched sides from a Spanish to a Mexican army in the middle of a battle, Santa Anna would have been incapable of understanding how or why the man had sacrificed his political career championing the rights of poor, landless settlers in his state.

Nor could he, who commanded respect by force and fear, have imagined this man's ability to win people over with his anecdotal "down-home" humor, which would establish an American tradition followed by people such as Abraham Lincoln, Mark Twain, and Will Rogers.

The forty-year-old officer, who carried a $7,000 sword into battle, would have shaken his head in disbelief to know that this backwoodsman, who had spent his whole life in debt, had once returned the loan of one dollar to the widow of a man who had given him the money ten years earlier. And Santa Anna, who was sometimes called the "Napoléon of the West," would have laughed had he known that this simple man lived by a personal credo of "Be always sure you are right and then go ahead."

As the conqueror of the Alamo ordered his men to burn the bodies of their enemies, he remained blind to the fact that his merciless policy would help elevate these men to an American Valhalla—and that the man lying in the dust at his feet did not become a hero simply because of the place and manner of his death.

Santa Anna may have learned his name, but he could never have known the man—David Crockett, American hero.

The Fifth Son

On August 17, 1786, Rebecca Hawkins Crockett, a young woman from Joppa, Maryland, gave birth to her fifth of nine children. Her husband, John Crockett, a former constable of Greene County, North Carolina, and now a struggling land speculator, stood by and looked on with pride. For poor, trans-Appalachian settlers, a birth amounted to another mouth to feed, but the new baby was the couple's fifth son in just six years of marriage, and sons always proved to be an asset on the frontier.

The child first saw the light of day in a log cabin located near a place where Limestone Creek flows into the Nolichucky River in what would someday be Greene County, Tennessee. He was named David, after John Crockett's father, who along with John's mother was killed by Creek Indians just eight years earlier.

As with most pioneer families, the Crocketts suffered poverty but not destitution. There was little hard currency nor the means to obtain it on the Western frontier, but while money was scarce, violence and danger were commonplace. The child's grandparents were slaughtered only three miles from where he lay in his crib. One of David's uncles suffered wounds and was left for dead in the attack, while another, who was deaf and mute, became a prisoner of the Creeks. David's father and uncle discovered the missing brother almost eighteen years later and were able to return him to his family after buying him back from the Indians.

David's parents had been married only a few months when, in October 1780, John left home and family to go to war. He was one of the "over the mountain men" of volunteer militia assembled to meet the British at the Battle of Kings Mountain, South Carolina rather than have the Redcoats "lay their country to waste with fire and sword" as promised if they did not swear their loyalty to the crown. The October 7 battle resulted in a resounding victory for the Patriots and turned the tide of the American Revolution in the South. The stories of redoubtable militiamen must have been recounted many times in the Crockett cabin over the years.

The elder Crockett provided for his family by means of his hunting rifle and supplemented the family income as a constable. In 1794 he began construction of a mill on Cove Creek, Tennessee, with a partner, and their plans were going along well until a flood ruined the enterprise. Years later David described it as "the second epistle to Noah's fresh, and away went the mill, shot, lock, and barrel."

The boy grew up with the rough-and-tumble companionship of four older brothers—no surer path to toughness and resiliency. Of the many adventures in which the five became involved, without the constraints of civilization, one was later described by Crockett as among his earliest memories.

The four older Crockett boys, and a fifteen-year-old friend named Campbell, were playing by the riverside with David tagging along. The older boys decided to set out on a river adventure in their father's canoe with David left unceremoniously onshore. Being older than the Crocketts, Campbell demanded the paddle despite the fact that he had no experience handling the craft, as the others did. Soon the canoe was out of control and heading for a set of falls—stern first. David watched the drama unfold, a bit smugly, after being left behind. What caused him to shriek in fear "like a young painter [panther]," as he would remember, was the sight of a neighbor, Amos Kendall, running toward him and tearing off his clothes like a madman.

David froze in fear as the man rushed by him and plunged into the river clad only in his breeches. Kendall overtook the canoe at a point twenty to thirty feet from the falls and wrestled it to shore against the pounding current. Close to becoming the only Crockett son, David was relieved that his brothers were safe but took some satisfaction at seeing that they were considerably more frightened than he.

Another of David's childhood memories pointed toward the unpredictability of life on the frontier. His uncle Joseph Hamilton was out deer hunting when he spied some movement in a thicket. To a hungry hunter this commotion apparently translated to food, and so without further investigation Uncle Joe promptly shot a Crockett neighbor who was gathering grapes. David remembered his father treating the wound by drawing a silk handkerchief through it, from one side of the body to the other. Years later, David reckoned that the neighbor "didn't fancy the business of gathering grapes in an out-of-the-way thicket soon again."

After the flood destroyed his mill, John Crockett moved his family to a rented home in Jefferson County, Tennessee. Two years later, in 1796, he set himself up as the proprietor of a tavern serving freighters and wagoners on the road linking Knoxville and Abingdon, Virginia.

Childhood was of short duration in the Tennessee wilderness. In 1798, a man by the name of Jacob Siler stopped at the Crockett tavern in the process of moving from Knox County, Tennessee, to Rockbridge, Virginia, taking with him his considerable stock of cattle. In a conversation with John Crockett, Siler said he could use some help driving the stock and suddenly twelve-year-old David found himself "hired to the old Dutchman, to go four-hundred miles on foot, with a perfect stranger that I never had seen until the evening before." Thus David Crockett, so associated with the history of the American West, earned his first money as a nascent "cowboy."

He reached Siler's destination, fulfilling his service, and for his labors earned the lofty sum of five or six dollars. He looked forward to starting back to his family but Siler did not want to let him go. The "Dutchman" was impressed by the hardworking boy, to whom he did not have to pay adult wages and who was amenable to orders, having been "taught so many lessons of obedience" by his father.

David spent the next few weeks with Siler, homesickness gnawing at him, until an opportunity presented itself. While playing by a roadside with two other youths, he recognized a Mr. Dunn, a regular at the Crockett tavern, who with his sons was driving three wagons to Knoxville. The wagoners listened to David's situation and offered a solution. The Dunns were staying the night at a tavern about seven miles from Siler's place. If the boy could get to the tavern before daylight he could join them on a route that would take him home.

David returned excitedly to Siler's that Sunday evening and secretly gathered together his clothing and money. At three hours before dawn he slipped out of the house and found about eight inches of snow covering the ground. Now he was faced with a choice: he could slip back into the warmth and safety of the Siler home, or he could go ahead with the plan to reach his family. For the latter, all he had to do was take a 225-mile wagon ride, and to reach the wagons he had to walk seven miles through calf-deep snow and a driving storm, at night, and alone. He reached the Dunns an hour before dawn, and after a breakfast by a warming fire was on the road heading back to Tennessee.

The wagons, plodding along through the snow, proved agonizingly slow for a boy stricken with homesickness, and at Roanoke, Virginia, the snail's pace became too much for him. After spending the night at the house of a man named John Cole, and despite the arguments of his benefactor Dunn, David set out on foot early in the morning and was well on his way when he ran into a bit of luck. He was overtaken on the road by a man returning from market with a drove of horses, one of which happened to be bridled and saddled. The boy gratefully accepted the offered ride that would save him miles on foot, and the trouble of wading the icy Roanoke River. Years later Crockett could not remember the gentleman's name but he never forgot the kindness extended to him—it was one of a number of serendipitous meetings throughout his life that helped him along in times of trouble. His ride left him a scant fifteen miles from his father's tavern, a distance he covered on foot.

Crockett's parents recognized the need for at least a rudimentary education for their children, and so, in the autumn of 1799, they enrolled David in the country school of one Benjamin Kitchen, near present-day Russellville, Tennessee. Everything went well in school until David had a confrontation with a boy older and larger than himself. With four older brothers he could have taken an easy way out but one late afternoon, while the older students were busy learning their spelling words, he slipped out of school early and waited. When his nemesis and cronies approached, David leaped from the cover of some bushes and attacked, giving the older boy "salt and vinegar" until his foe cried out for "quarters."

When he returned home he began to ponder the potential consequences of his actions. He got it into his head that schoolmaster Kitchen would take him to task if he returned to class, and rather than risk a whipping equal to or better than the one he had just doled out, he came to a simple solution: he just would not return to school. For the next several mornings he left for school with his brothers, somehow managed to convince the others to cover for him while he hid in the woods all day, then rejoined them on their walk home. Finally, the inevitable note from the teacher found its way into the hands of Crockett, Senior. He later said that his father had been "taking a few horns, and was in a good condition to make the fur fly," and while David explained his fears of being whipped by the schoolteacher, his father warned that he could expect a better whipping at home if he did not start for school immediately.

He did set out for school, but a little too sluggishly for his father's taste. The next thing the boy knew his father was after him with a sturdy hickory switch, and closing fast. Caught between the hammer of his father and the anvil of schoolmaster

Kitchen, David ran down a road leading away from school, which must have infuriated his father more. The race continued for about a mile until young Crockett crested a hill and hid in the underbrush. His father passed him, eventually gave up the chase, and returned to his cabin.

This episode is loved by modern writers on Crockett's life due to the "Daddy Dearest" image of a boy under the thumb of a violent and alcoholic father. There is no evidence, however, that John Crockett drank any more or less than his contemporaries, especially those in the tavern business. Nor is there any evidence that he subjected his children to more physical discipline than any other late-eighteenth-century frontier father. Crockett's autobiography makes no mention of any actual beatings, and it is likely that his father wielded the hickory switch more as an incentive than a weapon.

Whether or not David had experienced any switchings before, he found it beneficial not to test those waters on the occasion of his truancy. He went neither home nor to school, but instead made his way to the home of a man named Jesse Cheek who was about to start for Virginia with a drove of cattle, and with one of the older Crockett brothers already signed on, David also joined up.

The drive broke up in the town of Front Royal, Virginia, about a hundred miles west of Baltimore, where the cattle were sold. Always restless, David started on the return trip almost immediately, setting out with Cheek's brother on a single horse, leaving his own brother to follow with the rest of the company. After three days, however, the partnership ended when David realized that his companion was doing most of the riding, while he was doing most of the walking. Cheek went on alone with the horse after giving young Crockett four dollars to cover expenses for the almost 375-mile return trip.

On the road and on his own once again, David trudged along until he met a wagoner named Adam Myers. The two exchanged pleasantries and David learned that Myers was on his way north to Gerardstown, Virginia, and then would head back to Tennessee. They parted company and David started for home again but his thoughts turned to his father and schoolmaster Kitchen. He was certain that his father's anger would "hang on to him like a turtle does a fisherman's toe" so decided it would be safer to hire on with Myers, thus allowing for a longer cooling-off period back home.

After two days with Myers, he met up with his brother again. The older boy tried to persuade David to return home with him, invoking the love of his mother and sisters, but the youngster's mind was made up, and the Crockett boys bid each other a tearful farewell.

Once the freight was delivered to Gerardstown, Myers continued on to Alexandria, Virginia, for another load while David remained behind to wait for him, taking on work as a farmhand at twenty-five cents per day.

In the spring of 1800, he outfitted himself with new clothes bought with his earnings, and decided to make the run to Baltimore with Adam Myers. He was excited and curious to see what a real city and its people were like. As they approached Baltimore, he climbed into the wagon among the freight of heavy flour barrels to change into his newly bought finery. In the back he could not have seen the crew of wheelbarrow men working on the road but the wagon's horses did see them, spooked, and careened in the opposite direction. The wagon's tongue and both axles snapped, and David was tossed about the wagon like a rag doll among the barrels. Miraculously, he emerged from the wreckage unscathed, one of the first of many episodes in which he would either cheat death or return after he had been given up for dead. He took the whole thing philosophically, later writing, "If a fellow is born to be hung, he will never be drowned."

The two freighters hauled their cargo to Baltimore in another wagon and brought the wreck in for repairs. Meantime, David had time to explore the city, and made his way to the harbor, looking spellbound at the ships at dockside and those putting out to sea under sail. He never had seen such wonders before and at length mustered up enough courage to board one vessel. The captain, recognizing a sturdy-looking lad, invited him to sign on for the voyage to London. The opportunity captivated the adventurous boy and with the creaking deck rolling pleasantly beneath his feet, he contemplated the expanse of the Atlantic and agreed to go.

He returned to Myers, informed the wagoner of his plans to ship out, and requested his clothing and money. He could not have been prepared for the reaction: Myers not only adamantly refused to let David go but made a virtual prisoner of him until he was ready to take to the freight road again. He rejoined Myers under protest and under the constant threat of a bullwhip, but after several days he'd had enough, gathered his clothes, and lit out one morning before daybreak.

This time his journey was short-lived. After tramping only a few miles he met up with another wagoner heading west. He was Henry Myers of Pennsylvania (no relation to Adam Myers, from whom David had just made his getaway), and the man spoke to him in a kindly manner, asking his destination and how he came to be on the road on his own. David broke down in tears as he told of his plight.

Henry Myers turned out to be a tough and righteous man. He took David in hand and set out to find Adam Myers, resolving to retrieve the boy's money or take it out of his namesake's hide. After traveling two miles they found the other wagoner and the confrontation took place, with Henry accusing Adam of mistreating the boy. Adam laid the blame at David's feet. Henry demanded the seven dollars. This cowed Adam, who finally admitted he had spent the money, swearing he intended to repay it when he returned to Tennessee. This admission satisfied David and he persuaded his benefactor to drop the issue.

He traveled with Henry Myers for a few days but he resolved to press on to Tennessee on his own, and on the night before they parted company, Myers explained David's situation to a group of freighters, who passed the hat and collected three dollars. The next morning he set out, with his clothes and the money, for the rest of his life remembering the kindness of Henry Myers.

Very few paths that Crockett followed in his life were direct, and this one was no exception. At Montgomery Court House in Virginia he lingered for a month, working at odd jobs and earning five dollars. Afterward, he bound himself to Elijah Griffith, a hatter, for a term of four years but lasted only eighteen months when the business foundered and Griffith decamped without paying his employee.

Once again David found himself with no money, very few clothes, "and them very indifferent ones," and no prospects. He drifted, working a variety of minor jobs, until he was able to obtain some better garments and a small stake. So supplied he began his final push toward Tennessee.

At a place called New River, near present-day Radford in southwestern Virginia, he met yet another obstacle on the road home. The weather turned bad and the Little River fork of New River churned with whitecaps so treacherously that he could not induce anyone to ferry him across. Undeterred, he sought a canoe to cross on his own. He ignored the locals, who tried to explain the dangers and talk him out of it, found the boat, tied his clothes down, turned the craft upriver to battle the current and wind, and dug in with his paddle. After about two miles he reached the opposite shore, his clothes frozen to his skin and the canoe half filled with water. A three-mile hike brought him to a house, where he warmed himself before a roaring fire and with a little of the "creater [creature]" supplied by his surprised host. He had accomplished what the locals, experienced on the river, feared to do. David later described his river experience as "a mighty ticklish business, I tell you."

Upon finally arriving in Tennessee he visited his older brother, with whom he had started the cattle drive years before, and lingered with him for several weeks, apparently reluctant to complete his journey home. Eventually he began the last push and late one evening arrived at the Crockett tavern.

The reunion turned out to be joyful and emotional. Not yet fifteen years old, he had all but been given up for lost. All his fears of the long-dreaded switching disappeared when he saw the tears of his father. He remembered later being humbled by the reaction of his family and said that he would rather have submitted to a hundred whippings than have caused them so much anxiety.

Soon after his return his father came to him with a proposition. John Crockett was in debt to a man named Abraham

Wilson, owing Wilson thirty-six dollars. Despite David's independent adventures on the road, he was still a child in his father's household and John told him that if he worked off the debt to Wilson, David would be free as his own man. It must have been humbling for his father to come to his son with such a request; the boy had grown up during his two-year absence, and the days of hickory switch–induced races down the road clearly were over.

David unquestioningly took on the task, working for Wilson for six months without missing a single day. It is not known what type of work he performed but whatever it was, he earned enough to pay his father's note. He was now free of responsibility and recognized as a man by his family.

He next took employment with John Kennedy, a former North Carolinian who lived fifteen miles from the Crockett tavern. The man was a Quaker, whose working environment was a bit cleaner and calmer than Wilson's. David contracted to work for two shillings a day but at the end of his first week, Kennedy surprised him by presenting a note for forty dollars he held against John Crockett. Since David had been emancipated he could have shrugged off the debt but instead agreed to work off the note, foregoing the daily two shillings he could have earned.

He worked steadily for another six months, never once returning to visit his parents; when he did return to the Crockett tavern, he saw a look of fear and sorrow on his father's face when David presented the Kennedy note. The elder Crockett thought his son was serving as an agent of Kennedy's to collect the debt, but when David explained that it had been paid in full, his father burst into tears.

He visited his parents for a single day before returning to

work for Kennedy in order to buy some new clothing. He had been laboring for a solid year and had not accumulated a penny for himself.

He worked for two months until confronted with a problem totally outside his range of experience: love smote him in the form of a young Quaker girl, Kennedy's niece. This was something new to him. Painfully shy, his heart would "flutter like a duck in a puddle" whenever he tried to speak to her. Finally, when he did muster enough courage to approach her, he professed his love, assuring her he would "pine down to nothing" if he could not have her. The young woman patiently explained that she was engaged to be married.

The news devastated him, but ever the realist and a gentleman, he knew that there was nothing he could do about it. He began to search his soul for an explanation for his bad luck. He was an honest, sturdy, hardworking young man. The only thing lacking in his life was a formal education. There lay the answer.

It happened that Kennedy had a married son who lived nearby and ran a school. David made a deal with the young man to work for him for two days a week in return for four days of schooling a week plus board. He worked steadily, attended the school for six months, and mastered the basics of reading, writing, and arithmetic.

Love had set him on his path and after six months of schooling, the only education he would ever have, he determined that he'd had enough and pursued a prospective mate as purposefully and methodically as he would if on a hunt. He located a family of young, pretty girls he had known since childhood, and launched himself at one of them. He and the young woman, whose name he never revealed, courted and picked out a date to be married, or at least David thought they had. The eighteen-year-old boy looked forward to becoming the "happiest man in the created world, or in the moon, or any where else." So optimistic was he that neither he nor his intended bride bothered to mention their wedding plans to the girl's parents.

At about this same time he developed another interest that was destined to become more closely associated with him than romance. He managed to save up enough money to buy his first rifle, "a capital one," he said, and his attachment to it led to a love for shooting matches. Since these involved a demonstration of skill with the firearm for which a prize, usually a beef, was awarded, it amounted to a form of gambling. John Kennedy, with whom he had returned to live and work, looked on such activity with a jaundiced eye. David, along with a boy of his age who was bound to service with Kennedy, had to sneak out of the house to attend these matches. They cut a long pole and rested it against the upper story of the house where they slept and used it to shinny down. Sometimes they simply slipped out of the house, other times they would make a pretense of going deer hunting and head off for the matches. They had another, stronger incentive to steal away, however. David wanted to see his betrothed, and his companion had developed an attraction for one of her sisters, both living ten miles distant.

David managed to combine his two indulgences. One Saturday, after convincing Kennedy that he was going out after deer, he headed straight for his loved one, but stopped at a shooting match on the way, teaming up with a partner for the contest. They won the beef easily; he sold his share for five dollars and set off happily for the girl he planned to marry on that Thursday. However, in keeping with his meandering style, he stopped at the home of the girl's uncle on the way and there learned that the girl had been deceiving him, and that she was planning to marry someone else. He described this revelation as a "clap of thunder of a bright sunshiny day," and "the capstone of all the afflictions I had ever met with." Humiliated, he became convinced that he had been "born odd, and should always remain so, and that nobody would have me." He returned to the Kennedy's house and lapsed into luxurious self-pity for days.

When at last he shook off his love-induced lethargy he took up his rifle and went hunting. While he had not entirely given up on romance, he managed to resist the advances of the daughter of a Dutch widow. Part of his restraint was the fact that while the girl was intelligent and amiable, she was, he recalled, "as ugly as a stone fence." Still, he and the young lady cultivated a friendship. He was able to confide in her as to the type of wife he was looking for and his doubts about ever finding the right one. Once his confidante realized that she was out of the running she took on the role of matchmaker, invited David to a reaping, and requested he bring along any of his friends. If he did so she promised she would introduce him to a very pretty young woman. He returned to John Kennedy, and offered to work two days for him if he would allow his friend, the boy bound to Kennedy, to accompany him. The Quaker refused and admonished David not to go either. David went alone; he had promised the Dutch girl he would be there. More important, he could not pass up the chance of meeting the pretty girl.

Polly Finley *was* pretty. She remained out of sight just long enough after David's arrival to make an entrance. After introductions the two spent the evening chatting and dancing reels. He enjoyed himself, but must have begun wondering whether

he was the hunter or the hunted when Polly's mother began referring to him as her "son-in-law." He wisely played along. To
him it was just so much "salting the cow to catch the calf."

He began to court Polly in earnest but to his chagrin soon
discovered that Mrs. Finley was not sold on having him as a
son-in-law after all; in fact, she favored another young man.
During one weekend David found himself and his rival court-
ing Polly at the same time. Only his dogged persistence, and
the fact that Polly obviously preferred his company, drove the
other suitor away. He stayed at the Finley home with Polly and
her parents until Monday morning and then headed home. He
would not see her again for several weeks.

In the interim a great wolf hunt, to be conducted in sparsely
populated woods that were unfamiliar to him, occupied his attention. It was a sunny day when the hunters fanned out
through the woods. He was having a grand time, so grand, in
fact, that he barely noticed the clouds rolling in, obscuring the
sun, and along with it any reference to compass points or direction. When he finally realized this, the young man who would
be forever remembered as one of America's greatest frontiersmen found himself alone, lost in the woods, and scared. He
wandered around seeking some landmark without any luck.
(He later developed a theory from his plight, and passed it on
for the benefit of other hunters. "Whenever a fellow gets bad
lost," he wrote, "the way home is just the way he don't think it
is.") His chances of finding his way out were dimming along
with the daylight when his uncanny luck during times of trouble returned. In the late-afternoon light he saw a young woman
running through the trees and gave chase, hoping she could
lead him out of the woods. When the woman finally became

aware of his presence she stopped and waited for him. It was none other than Polly Finley, who had been out chasing down her father's horses, but had become as lost as David. Now, at least, they were lost together. They searched until they found a path, came to a house just at nightfall, and under the supervision of their hosts, spent the rest of the night planning their future. In the morning they went their separate ways but made a date to get together in one month.

In the meantime, he went back to work to pay off the balance on his horse and to begin to use his rifle to supplement his income. It was important for him to clear up his debts and accumulate funds since at their next meeting he and Polly planned to set a date for their marriage. He made plans for a wedding party at the Crockett tavern, then returned to Polly's house to ask the Finleys for her hand in marriage. Polly's father was amenable to the proposal, but her mother's attitude was not so benevolent. David found his prospective mother-in-law to be "mighty wrathy." She looked at him "as savage as a meat ax" and threw him out of the house.

He'd had enough. There was to be no more "salting the cow." Over Mrs. Finley's protestation he told Polly that he would be back on the following Thursday with a horse, bridled and saddled for her. On the way back to his father's tavern he stopped by a local preacher's house and made arrangements for the marriage.

On a Thursday in August 1806, he set out with two of his brothers, a sister, a sister-in-law, and two friends. Near Polly's home they were met by a large group who planned to attend the wedding. David remained behind with his sister and one friend and sent the rest of the party on ahead. After a while, some of the young men speeded back to him with a flask filled with liquor by Polly's father. This ritualistic act was a clear signal of welcome and acceptance on the part of his future father-in-law. The news of Mrs. Finley, however, was not so encouraging. She remained dead set against the union but David had made up his mind. He rode up to the Finleys' door, refused to dismount, and invited Polly to come out and ride away with him.

Mr. Finley could not let Polly elope before his very eyes and those of his friends so he put himself in the embarrassing position of having to address young Crockett, who was on horseback, while he himself was on foot. He used every argument to persuade David to stay and marry Polly in her home. He even admitted that his wife had a little too much to say in the matter. David's determination began to crack; he agreed to remain and do things properly under the condition that Polly's mother come out and ask him to do so herself. Mother Finley did emerge from the house, apologized, and invited him to stay. At last they summoned the preacher and the wedding took place. A reception followed at the Finleys' and then another on the following day at the Crockett tavern. David now had his own horse, his own rifle, and a beautiful wife. For a free nineteen-year-old man in the Tennessee backwoods he felt as though he "needed nothing more in the whole world."

The Volunteer

The Crocketts began their life together with a wedding gift of two cows and calves from the Finleys, and a voucher from John Kennedy allowing Polly to buy fifteen dollars' worth of goods at a local store. They rented a plot of land not far from his parents, where David farmed and Polly took on all the chores of a frontier wife, performing them expertly. David was particularly proud of her ability as a weaver, which he attributed to her Irish background.

Soon the realities and responsibilities of married life began to sink in. He quickly learned that laboring over the unforgiving earth "wan't the thing it was cracked up to be," and found that he was paying what he considered to be unreasonably high rent for the privilege. Before settling down he had wandered as he pleased, making enough money to cover his needs. Now, he found himself tied to an unyielding little piece of land that he did not own, with little chance of showing a profit for his labors. In addition, he and Polly had two sons in their first three years of marriage, John Wesley, born on July 10, 1807, and William, on November 25, 1809. Crockett liked to remark that he was "better at increasing my family than my fortune."

He thought that as long as he had to work as a farmer it made sense for him to do so on a better piece of land. To follow this line of thought, he tied much of his and Polly's worldly goods on the backs of two young colts, and headed 150 miles west to Lincoln County, so named for the Revolutionary War hero General Benjamin Lincoln. The richness of the land on the Mulberry Fork of the Elk River did not satisfy David as much as the abundance of game. In this wild paradise he earned his lifelong reputation as a hunter and not so humbly remembered that in this skill "lay the foundation for all my future greatness."

He and his family remained in the country for only two years before relocating on Bean's Creek in Franklin County, ten miles below Winchester, Tennessee. On November 25, 1812, Polly gave birth to a daughter, Margaret.

That year, when the young United States again went to war against Great Britain, David and his fellow frontiersmen were far from the action but had military concerns of their own. A year earlier, Tecumseh, the warrior-statesman, and his brother, Tenskwatawa the Prophet, of the Shawnee Indian tribe, attempted to foment a revolt of the Southeastern tribes—the Creeks, Chickasaws, and Choctaws—against American settlers. Tecumseh was killed and the revolt ultimately failed, but the Indian threat continued. In 1812, the British allied themselves with the tribes by arming them against the United States.

During the summer of 1813 a band of almost two hundred white men ambushed a party of Creek Indians at a place called

Burnt Corn Creek in southern Alabama. On the surface it was preemptive action since the whites feared the Indians had obtained weapons and powder from the Spanish in Pensacola, Florida. Although outnumbered, the Creeks rallied and drove off their inept attackers.

On August 30, 1813, the Indian band retaliated by attacking Fort Mims, southwest and down the Alabama River from Burnt Corn Creek. Two hundred eighty-eight civilians had taken refuge there, "protected" by about 265 militiamen called the Mississippi Volunteers. The Creeks found the stockade gates invitingly open, and many of the volunteers socializing with the young civilian women. Major Daniel Beasley, in command of the militiamen, unsuccessfully tried to close the gates and was killed in the process. When the feeble resistance ended, the attackers systematically slaughtered close to five hundred men, women, and children. A few others escaped and a few were taken captive. This was the opening battle of the First Creek War.

Crockett and his family lived in midsouth Tennessee, just above the Alabama border, when the tales of the attack on Fort Mims reached them and their neighbors. The War of 1812 had spread west of the Appalachians.

Despite his later reputation, Crockett was not a warrior or even a particularly violent person. However, when he learned about Fort Mims he felt he had to volunteer for service against the Creeks. Polly tried to dissuade him from going off to war, leaving her in an unfamiliar place with their three children, and with no certainty that the Indian attacks would not reach her. Crockett knew this, but determined that it would be better to seek out and fight them many miles distant than on his doorstep, and Polly had been with him long enough to know that he could not be deterred. He told her, "If every man would wait till his wife got willing for him to go to war, there would be no fighting done, until we would all be killed in our own houses." He also believed that going to war was "a duty I owed my country," and later related that he had often heard war described, but admitted that he "verily believed in my own mind, that I couldn't fight in that way at all." Some historians have interpreted this statement to mean that Crockett was against warfare, and did not really want to participate in it. More likely, however, he referred to the *manner* of organized battle, in which opposing armies stood in ranks and fired volleys at each other at almost point-blank range. To a frontiersman this was the greatest of follies. Whatever his thoughts on war in general, he joined the muster of volunteers, surprised to find that he did not feel the "dread of dying" that he had expected.

He and other civilian volunteers gathered in the town of Winchester, Tennessee, about ten miles from his home. There, Francis Jones, a lawyer from the town who would later serve as a Tennessee congressman, addressed the men as he walked in front of their assembled ranks. He announced that he was raising his own company and invited any who wished to join him to step forward. He also explained to them their right as volunteers to elect their own officers. Only one or two stepped out of ranks before Crockett. Then others followed, forming Jones's company of Tennessee Volunteer Mounted Riflemen.

After the organization, Crockett found time to return home and provide for Polly and the boys, while she helped equip him with what little he needed for his expedition. He did not expect to be gone long and did not burden himself with an excess of gear, reasoning that if he did join in battle with the Creeks it would be beneficial not to be "pestered with any unnecessary plunder, to prevent my having a fair shake with them."

He returned to Winchester, marched with the volunteers past the town of Huntsville, Alabama, and set up camp at an assembly point called Beaty's Spring. After a few days there were as many as thirteen hundred mounted men gathered at the spring, and as the numbers grew so did Crockett's confidence and pride in the men. "I verily believe the whole army was of the real grit," he later wrote. Captain Jones addressed his men several times, reminding them of what lay ahead and, since they had as yet not been mustered in, advised them that they could go home if they did not feel up to the task. None of the men backed out. Crockett probably spoke for all of them when he later admitted that he "felt wolfish all over."

His enlistment began on September 24, 1813, a commitment of ninety days, his company a part of the Second Regiment of Tennessee Volunteers under the command of Colonel John Coffee, a frontier planter, merchant, and crony of the force's overall commander, General Andrew Jackson.

Before long David was put to work. Coffee's subordinate, Major John H. Gibson, approached Francis Jones and requested two men for a scouting expedition, specifying that he needed the two best woodsmen and riflemen that the captain could spare. Jones recommended Crockett, who asked permission to choose the second scout. The major agreed, but regretted his decision when Crockett chose a young man—actually little more than a boy—named George Russell. Gibson showed his displeasure, stating that he needed men, not boys, for his expedition, pointing out that Russell did not have enough beard to qualify. But Crockett had confidence in his young friend's ability, and unimpressed by the officer's authority, stated that courage should not be measured by a beard "for fear a goat would have preference over a man." The major needed Crockett's skills and gave in. The expedition set off with Gibson taking ten men, plus Crockett and Russell, with him.

The thirteen crossed the Tennessee River in northern Alabama at a place called Ditto's Landing and traveled less than ten miles before camping for the night. Crockett later recalled proudly that he was "one of the first men that ever crossed the Tennessee River into the Creek War." The following morning the party split up, one group with Gibson and the other under Crockett, to find the houses of the Cherokees Dick Brown and his father. Their purpose was to gather as much intelligence as they could on the Creeks, then meet at a designated crossroads fifteen miles beyond the Browns' homes. Crockett did not obtain any useful information from the elder Brown, but did enlist the aid of a half-blood Cherokee who agreed to meet him and his party at the crossroads that night. He told his new recruit to hoot like an owl when he got to the roads. The party concealed themselves in a hollow near the meeting place and at about ten that night the Cherokee announced his presence with his owl call. Gibson and the men of his party had as yet not rejoined the others.

By the next morning, with no useful information to bring back to the army, and Gibson still unaccounted for, Crockett and the others pushed on twenty miles to a Cherokee town, then into the very borders of the Creek nation itself. There they visited and took dinner with a jittery white man named Radcliff who was married to a Creek woman. The man explained that a war party of Creeks, painted for business, had passed his place not an hour before. He also explained that if the warriors found out that militia were visiting him, there would be little hope for him or his family. Radcliff's uneasiness spread to some of the men, a few of them voicing the opinion that it might be a good idea to get back to their home base. Crockett would not give in to their fears. He said that they would never hear the end of it from the others in camp if they returned now. They were out there to do a job, and he did not intend to go back until he had accomplished it. There were only six of them but he knew that some would stick with him, and that the others were too afraid to start back on the trail alone.

He and his men began their search for the hostiles under the light of a nearly full moon, their destination the camp of some friendly Creeks, eight miles distant. On the way they met up with two black men, brothers who were in the unique act of escaping from their Creek captors in order to return to their white slave masters. They were well mounted, and Crockett sent one back to the point where he and his men had crossed the Tennessee River; the other he had join his party.

About forty men, women, and children occupied the Creek camp. The white men easily fell in with them in a somewhat tense atmosphere. The escaped slave, who could speak the Creek language, learned that the Indian men of the camp were understandably worried that if the war party discovered the white men's presence, the whole camp would be wiped out. Crockett, unimpressed, whiled away his time practicing archery with some boys by the illumination of a pine light. When the black man pressed the concerns of the Creek villagers, Crockett told them that he would keep watch and if a hostile appeared he would "carry the skin of his head home to make me a mockasin."

The villagers were reassured to some extent and laughed at the cocky white man's reply, but he and his men still slept with their rifles in their arms, their horses saddled and ready by their sides, "if in the night our quarters should get uncomfortable," Crockett said.

Things quickly became uncomfortable. A high-pitched shriek tore through the camp and scrambled the volunteers from their bedrolls. The cry came from a friendly Indian runner who roused the camp, shouting that the Creek "Red Sticks" (so called because of the painted war clubs they carried) were on the move. He reported that the hostiles had crossed the Coosa River at a place called Ten Islands, near present-day Gadsden, Alabama, and were headed for the main force of General Andrew Jackson's army. The news caused pandemonium in the camp and the friendly Creeks disappeared in minutes. Crockett resolved that his duty was to warn the army, so he and his men set off on the sixty-five miles back to Ditto's Landing.

After an exhausting night the scouting party reached the camp at ten in the morning and there Crockett reported to Colonel Coffee with the news. Coffee reacted to the report with a bored indifference, which caused the Tennessean to begin "burning inside like a tar kiln." He had expected the whole camp to spring to life with his news but the only reaction was the posting of a double guard that night. On the following morning the missing Major Gibson returned to camp with his party and reported to Coffee, telling the colonel the same story that Crockett had reported the day before. This time Coffee was put "all in a fidget" by the news, ordered a quarter-mile-long breastworks constructed, and sent a dispatch rider to General Jackson at Fayetteville, Alabama, a day's march distant.

Crockett concluded that his report was not believed because he was neither an officer nor a great man but "just a poor soldier." He failed to take into account that his report was based strictly on hearsay and that he had never actually seen the hostiles himself. However, he saw the whole business as an indication of an army caste system, and it became a sore spot that stayed tender the rest of his life.

General Jackson was not content to wait and let the Creeks make their move. He mobilized his infantry and after a grueling forced march, joined the cavalry force near the Tennessee River. While his infantry recuperated he sent the cavalry forward across the Tennessee, through Huntsville, Alabama, and then made a second crossing of the river, one that proved especially treacherous. A number of horses became hopelessly stuck in rock crevices in the two-mile-wide waterway and had to be abandoned.

At the site of the future town of Tuscaloosa, Jackson's men burned a deserted Indian village called Black Warrior's Town and appropriated its supply of corn, a fortunate acquisition since the force had exhausted its supply of meat. This parched corn proved less than palatable for a hunter, especially when the woods abounded in game, so Crockett asked Colonel Coffee permission to do a little hunting as they marched along. Coffee agreed and the first game he came upon was a deer, freshly killed and skinned by Indians. Food was so scarce that Crockett violated an unspoken rule of the wilderness—do not steal another hunter's kill, even an enemy's. He struggled back to camp with the appropriated meat and shared it with as many of his fellow soldiers as it would feed.

He fared better on the following day when he came upon a gang of wild hogs, bringing one down with his rifle and sending the others stampeding into the cavalry camp, which erupted in wild gunfire. When he returned with his kill, he found that the men had managed to bring down several other hogs, plus a stray cow, without killing one another.

The cavalry joined up briefly with Jackson's infantry on the following day before pushing on to Radcliff's place and finding the owner a little less friendly on this occasion—in fact, he had hidden away his provisions of potatoes and corn lest they fall into the hands of the army. Upon questioning Radcliff it developed that he had sent the screaming runner into Crockett's camp to spread a false alarm of the Red Sticks. In retribution, the volunteers pressed Radcliff's two grown sons into army service.

Crockett received his baptism of fire on November 3, 1813. John Coffee, who had been promoted to brigadier general only a few days earlier, had set up camp at Ten Islands, Alabama, and named it Fort Strother. Operating out of this base his scouts determined that the Creeks were encamped at a place called Tallusahatchee, about ten miles distant. Coffee and his force, numbering between nine hundred and a thousand men, approached the sleeping camp before daylight and surrounded the village. Captain Hammond and a company of rangers, frontier irregulars who operated in front of the main force, were sent forward but were spotted before they reached the camp. A cry of alarm split the morning and warriors boiled out to meet the threat. They pursued Hammond and his men back to the army's lines and exchanged a volley with Coffee's force before the warriors were driven back to their village. As the volunteers closed in, tightening the circle, many of the Indians saw the hopelessness of the situation and surrendered. Crockett remembered one volunteer beset by no less that seven Creek women all clinging to his hunting shirt and trying to surrender. He reported that all who sought to surrender were taken prisoner but not all chose to do so. He counted forty-six warriors who took refuge in one of the houses. As the militiamen approached they noticed a Creek woman sitting in the doorway, and before any of them could react she put her feet against a bow, fitted an arrow, pulled back with both hands, and let fly, killing a volunteer lieutenant. Crockett stood stunned, having never seen a man killed before. The incensed volunteers opened fire on the woman and riddled her with at least twenty balls. The fever of revenge spread through the ranks. He remembered, "We now shot them like dogs, and set the house on fire," but did not report if any of the forty-six warriors escaped. He watched as a boy of only about twelve years, whose arm and thigh had been shattered by gunfire, crawled so close to the flaming house that he set himself on fire. Crockett said that "not a murmur escaped him" and that the boy "had sooner die than make a noise, or ask for quarters."

The battle ended quickly. About 185 Creek warriors were killed or taken prisoner; eighty-four women and children were captured. Coffee lost five men killed. The slaughter at Tallusahatchee was regarded by General Jackson and many of his volunteers as balancing out the Fort Mims massacre.

The volunteers' attention now turned to their growing hunger. They had been on half rations for days, their supply of beef had run out long ago, and no provisions had reached them. Many had already taken to gnawing on beef hides. On the day following the battle, some of the men, including Crockett, drifted back to the scene of the slaughter. The blackened but recognizable bodies of Creek warriors, their limbs twisted and contorted, lay in the ruins. While poking around the scene someone discovered a well-stocked potato cellar under the house, the potatoes thoroughly cooked by the blaze, and generously basted by the burning bodies on the floor above. Hunger and horror balanced precariously before the starving volunteers, until the scales tipped toward hunger.

Four days after Tallusahatchee an Indian runner brought urgent news to General Jackson at Fort Strother. A force of Creeks, probably a thousand in number, had besieged Fort Leslie, the home and stockade of Alexander Leslie, a local trader, near Talladega, thirty miles southeast of Tallusahatchee. The hostile Creeks sought to enlist the aid of the Indians inside the fort against Jackson's forces. If they did not assist, they were told, the stockade would be taken by force, along with all the provisions and ammunition. Those inside stalled and sent messengers to Jackson begging for assistance. The general's camp, including Crockett's unit, mobilized and were on the trail within an hour of the arrival of the appeal.

Colonel Coffee's cavalrymen were sent forward to encircle the enemy while Jackson's infantry moved in from the front, but hostile scouts spotted them approaching. One cavalry company attempted to draw the Creeks out of hiding and bring the battle on, actually moving past the fort and, to the dismay of the men inside, toward a trap set by the Indians. No amount of frantic gestures and calls from the fort could warn the cavalrymen of the danger. Finally, two Indians from the fort jumped the walls, and forcibly took the bridle of the officer's horse. Immediately the Creeks opened fire and swarmed from their cover "like a cloud of Egyptian locusts," in Crockett's words. The forward party escaped only by abandoning their horses and scampering to the comparative safety of the stockade.

Meantime, the naked and red-painted warriors threw themselves against one point of Jackson's encircling force. A solid volley from the troops broke their charge and sent them reeling against another part of the circle. The Creeks fought back as best they could while volley after volley tore into them, the Indians finally hitting a weak spot in the line made up of untested militia draftees. The line buckled and almost seven hundred of the enemy escaped. Jackson was livid since the uprising could have been crushed had his men held. As it ended, some three hundred Creeks were killed, but more than enough lived to fight another day. Jackson's forces lost seventeen men killed and over eighty wounded.

After Tallusahatchee and Talladega, with winter approaching and supplies scarce, the volunteers became anxious to return home since their tours of duty were nearly over. There were some tense moments with the troops that might have resulted in open mutiny had not Jackson's force of will held them in check. Finally, the general begrudgingly allowed the men to return to their homes for a brief rest, to resupply with winter clothing and find fresh horses. The volunteers were furloughed on November 22 with the understanding that they would gather at Huntsville again on December 8.

Crockett returned home and replenished his family's food and firewood supply to sustain them during the last two weeks of his enlistment. Polly's unhappiness at seeing him depart again, after being home for only two weeks, did not deter him from returning to Huntsville and regrouping with the others.

Not all the volunteers were faithful to their pledge. Some reasoned that since they had only two weeks remaining of their enlistment, it made no sense to return. Many refused to return when word spread through the ranks that they were expected to complete an additional three months' service beyond their original agreement. Crockett became one of the few who decided to serve out his time. On December 24, after his enlistment ended, he stayed on with the army as a member of the scouting company of Major William Russell, the father of the young man who had accompanied him on his scouting expedition a year earlier.

On January 21, 1814, Crockett camped with Jackson's army at the Tallapoosa River, three miles from a large enemy camp at Emuckfau Creek. Two hours before dawn the camp erupted with the popping of rifle fire. As the Indians attacked, the volunteers built up their campfires then dropped back into the darkness, hoping the Creeks would charge into the light of the fires where they could be cut down. However, the enemy force refused to be drawn in and the two sides fell to blasting away at each other in the dark. The fight ended at daybreak when the Creeks finally faded away. The volunteers suffered four men killed and a number wounded. They buried their dead and burned a large pile of logs over the grave to prevent the Indians from returning and scalping the bodies.

Afterward, Jackson decided to move his army back to Fort Strother but on January 24, while the troops were in the process of crossing Enotochopco Creek, the enemy struck again. The general found his command split with the advance units on one side of the Enotochopco, and his rear guard and artillery on the other, at the mercy of the attackers. Some of the rear guard panicked and broke, leaving a volunteer artillery company isolated. While the cannoneers defended themselves in hand-to-hand combat, Colonel William Carroll, commanding the rear, rallied enough men to make a stand. Carroll was a trusted friend of Jackson's who would succeed him as major general of the militia in 1814. He bought enough time for his men and those of the wounded General Coffee to counterattack and ultimately drive the Creeks off. For a while the action was harrowing, striking Crockett as "hot as fresh mustard on a sore shin." He credited Carroll for saving the day, and admitted they would have been soundly beaten if it had not been for the colonel's actions. Crockett himself was rattled by the engagement and admitted that he was "mighty glad when it was over, and the savages quit us, for I had begun to think there was one behind every tree in the woods." He decided that he had "done Indian fighting enough for one time," and since another contingent of volunteers had joined the army, he obtained a furlough and headed home. In doing so he missed the decisive battle of Horseshoe Bend on March 28, 1814, in which Jackson destroyed the Creek forces once and for all.

The war against England continued, however, and while Crockett hunted and farmed along Bean's Creek, in August 1814, the Redcoats burned Washington, D.C. Within a month he reenlisted, to Polly's dismay, in order to get "a small taste of British fighting." When one of Crockett's neighbors, who had been drafted, heard of his eagerness to get into the fray, he offered a hundred dollars if David would go in his place. Crockett managed to resist the temptation of this phenomenal sum, explaining that he had been "better raised than to hire myself out to be shot at," and even offered the man a gentle lecture about how the country could use the services of both of them.

He enlisted again in a company commanded by Major William Russell, this time called the Separate Battalion of

Tennessee Mounted Gunmen. He entered his military service as a third sergeant, probably based on his record from the previous year and his friendship with Russell.

The Mounted Gunmen and Andrew Jackson's army headed for the Spanish possession of Pensacola in the western panhandle of Florida. There, the Spanish had allowed three hundred British troops to land for the purpose of training and arming renegade Creeks who had not adhered to the treaty ending the late war. Jackson intended to stem this threat to Mobile and New Orleans as well as punish the Spanish for violating their neutrality. Russell's company started on its route south through Alabama, falling two days behind Jackson's main force, Crockett passing across much of the same ground he had known the year before. Due to the lack of forage, the main army left its horses at a place called the Cut-off, not far from Fort Mims and about eighty miles from Pensacola. Russell's company followed suit upon reaching the Cut-off, proceeded on foot, still two days behind the others, and arrived at the army's camp at noon on November 8, 1814. Unfortunately, those who may have been anxious for a taste of "British fighting" were too late. Jackson had taken the town the day before after a halfhearted defense by the Spanish. Crockett and a few cronies drifted into town to take a "horn" of liquor and observe the British fleet, with its soldiers safely aboard, in the bay. By the next day, Russell's company was on its way back to Fort Montgomery, Alabama, near Fort Mims, there to resupply and prepare for a dangerous and debilitating hide-and-seek game with renegade Creeks in the swamps of south Alabama and west Florida. Meantime, Jackson and his army turned west toward New Orleans, where he would win everlasting fame in the greatest land battle of the war.

Another volunteer unit soon joined Major Russell's force, which was combined into a regiment commanded by regular army major Uriah Blue of Virginia. The troops supplied themselves with wild beef, formerly the property of the slaughtered residents of Fort Mims, and set off south back toward Pensacola. The force numbered approximately a thousand men, 186 of them Chickasaw and Choctaw Indians—two of the southeastern "civilized tribes," so called because they were quicker and more amenable to adopting white customs. The troops camped on the west side of the Escambia River and were lucky enough to receive such supplies as sugar, coffee, and liquor, brought in by boat to Pensacola.

The Indians under Russell were anxious to begin their scouting mission and offered to cross the river to set up camp on the east side. Russell agreed, going with them and taking Crockett and fifteen other of his volunteers along. In the morning the rest of the force crossed the river and began their hunt for the renegade Creeks. Much of the brushy countryside was chest-deep in water, and after reaching some pine-covered hills, Crockett and his advance scouts warmed themselves by a feeble fire before setting out again. That day news arrived about an enemy camp on an island nearby, information that excited the Chickasaws and Choctaws, who urged that the camp be attacked at once. Russell and his men moved out behind two of their enthusiastic scouts, and hurried forward to the sound of rifle shots. They found that their Indians had met and feigned friendship with two Creeks out hunting for their horses, then promptly murdered and beheaded them. In a horrific ritual, all the members of the Indian contingent took turns striking the severed heads with their war clubs. Crockett, caught up by the bizarre scene, joined in, after which he was surrounded by the Indians, who proclaimed him "warrior—warrior." Farther on, Crockett and his scouts discovered the scalped bodies of a Spanish couple and their four children. The brutal realities of the campaign were beginning to wear heavily on the army, and he admitted to feeling "mighty ticklish along about this time." When the party finally reached the island camp, the men found only two women and ten children, whom they captured.

Before the Indian scouts had murdered the two Creeks, they learned there was a larger enemy camp nine miles up the Conecuh River. Major Russell decided to proceed there, but Colonel Blue vetoed the plan and ordered the unit to return. Two companies skirmished with Creeks on their way back, taking many of them prisoner, Crockett later hearing that the prisoners were all killed and scalped by the "friendly" Indians who were entrusted to escort them to Fort Montgomery.

By January 1, 1815, the force under Uriah Blue had been on its mission for thirty-four days with minimal success, and with rations for only twenty days. The situation became so desperate that Blue and his men marched all night to attack a strong enemy town, hoping to find food there. Instead they found the town deserted and all the provisions gone. The volunteers burned the village and returned to camp with a hunger bordering on starvation.

With provisions becoming critical, the volunteer force split up with Russell's group headed for Fort Decatur on the Tallapoosa River. There they received one ration of meat apiece and continued to scout the countryside, finding nothing substantial to sustain them. Rather then sit idly around a campfire starving with his comrades, Crockett and a few companions ranged the countryside, hunting for three days with very little to show for their efforts, and were close to exhaustion when they chanced upon a prairie with the unmistakable signs of deer, bear, and turkey. Even with the promise of larger game, smaller food sources for the communal cook pot were not overlooked. At one point Crockett climbed thirty feet up a tree to retrieve a squirrel he had shot. Later two more squirrels and two large turkeys were shot, and the next day the hunters fared even better when Crockett brought down a fine buck. He and his partner brought their game back to camp just in time to prevent Captain William Russell, another son of old Major Russell, from shooting his horse to feed to the troops.

Besides hunting for food, Crockett bartered for it when necessary. After the disappointing fare at Fort Decatur, he traded with an Indian he had met ten charges of powder and ten bullets for two hats full of corn. The volunteers' mounts suffered too, and he witnessed thirteen good horses abandoned on one day because they were too weak to go on.

The debilitating winter campaign and frustration at the lack of success in subduing the Creeks had taken their toll. In early February 1815, Crockett had camped near Fort Strother when a fresh contingent of volunteers arrived from east Tennessee. Many of his neighbors and acquaintances were among their number, and it must have been a source of concern as well as pride to find his younger brother, John, with the new troops. After a few days the new men moved on to Mobile, leaving Crockett at Fort Strother, where he lingered for a while before taking a leave. He headed home, receiving a warm and loving reception from Polly and his children, but within days was called back into service to fulfill the month or so of his enlistment. He was ordered to the Black Warrior River country in Alabama to begin another hunt for hostile Creeks, but, after almost a year and a half of desultory soldiering, experiencing near starvation in the winter campaign and the brutality of frontier warfare, he'd had enough. He hired a willing young man to serve out his remaining month, returned home once again, and settled down with his family.

Sergeant David Crockett officially ended his military service in March 1815, with a new appreciation for home and family.

The Gentleman from the Cane

Crockett worked at his farm at Bean's Creek for the next two years. With the war behind him, these should have been peaceful times, but early in 1815, possibly even before he returned home, he lost his beloved Polly to an unidentified illness. Suddenly responsible for three small children and with a farm to tend, he sought the aid of his younger brother, John, also home safely from the war, and his wife. The two moved into his home and cared for the children while the grieving father, driven by loneliness and the need for a mother for his young ones, began to court Elizabeth Patton, a widow with two children of her own. Born on May 22, 1788, into a prominent North Carolina family, Elizabeth was raised there and married her cousin James Patton, thus retaining her maiden name, before moving with him to Tennessee. James died during service in the Creek War, the exact date and circumstances of his death uncertain.

In his autobiography, Crockett wrote of his interest in

Elizabeth with a teasing humor, obviously with an eye to the fact that she would be reading it, describing her as a "good industrious woman, and owned a snug little farm, and lived quite comfortable." Of his courtship style he likened it to "a fox when he is going to rob a hen-roost." They married at her family's home on her birthday in 1816. When a pig came snorting through the front door, interrupting the proceedings, the bridegroom led the uninvited guest out the door with the warning, "Old Hook, from now on, *I'll* do the grunting around here."

Crockett once again had a wife, and now five children, to provide for, and he and Elizabeth wasted no time in starting a "second crop together." Their first child's date of birth is listed as September 16, 1816, which causes some confusion and raised eyebrows in the chronology of Polly's death, his marriage to Elizabeth, and the birth of Robert Patton Crockett. Polly died in 1815, and some sources put Crockett's marriage to Elizabeth Patton in the summer of that year. Other sources put the second marriage in May 1816, meaning that Elizabeth gave birth within four months of the wedding. Either scenario is possible, as well as the possibility that Crockett and his second wife lived together in a common-law relationship before formalizing their union. Elizabeth had her own land holdings, superior to his, plus a tidy dowry of as much as eight hundred dollars, which they would use toward future relocations and enterprises.

With the burden of an ever-growing family, Crockett began to tire of his place on Bean's Creek, which he described as "sickly," so in the fall set out with three companions across the Tennessee River and into Creek territory to land recently made accessible after the late war. Misfortune plagued them from the start when, after traveling only a day, one of the men suffered a poisonous snakebite while hunting. He was left to recover at the house of a wartime acquaintance while the others traveled as far as Tuscaloosa and camped there. About two hours before dawn the explorers realized that their horses had run off, and Crockett inherited the job of rounding them up again. He spent the next day in pursuit, lugging his heavy rifle through swamps, creeks, and over mountains, never catching a glimpse of the animals, but encouraged by rumors of their passing at every homestead he visited. By nightfall he gave up, after traveling what he estimated to be an almost fifty-mile hunt, and sought lodging at the nearest house. In the morning he awoke to aches, pains, and fatigue so severe he had barely the strength to walk. Still, he felt obliged to try to rejoin his companions if only to let them know that he had been unable to retrieve the horses, and so set out again walking until afternoon, when he became so ill with a throbbing headache that he could not bear the weight of his rifle and collapsed at the side of the road.

Two passing Indians chanced upon him and tried to revive him by feeding him some ripe melon. When he proved too nauseated to eat, the Indians calmly told him in sign language that he would soon die. They told him of a house about a mile and a half away, and when he got on his feet, staggering about like a drunken man, he paid one of the Indians a dollar to help him along and carry his rifle. The owners of the house took him in, unsuccessfully tried to revive him with warm tea, and finally left him in feverish delirium for the rest of the night. The next morning two of Crockett's neighbors, also exploring the Creek territory, happened to find out about his plight and helped him return to his companions. However, by the time they had located his friends his condition had worsened and he could no longer sit up. The four carried him to another nearby house, left him with the owners, bought horses, and continued on their explorations without him.

Crockett writhed in fever for two weeks, unable to speak for one five-day stretch. His hosts were convinced he would die until the woman of the household tried one last remedy, dosing him with a whole bottle of a nostrum called Bateman Drops. The drops apparently worked since by the next morning his fever had broken, and he could speak again and take some sips of water. He could not have known it, but he had survived his first bout with malaria, most likely contracted while sloshing around the swamps of west Florida in search of the Creeks.

Once he regained his strength he hitched a ride with a wagoner returning home just twenty miles from the Crockett farm, borrowed one of the man's horses, and continued on. Elizabeth looked at him as if he were a ghost, not only from his loss of weight, pallor, and a face that looked like it had been "half soled with brown paper," but because she had given up on ever seeing him again. His original traveling companions had miraculously recovered their missing horses, returned his to Elizabeth, and told her they had met men who saw her husband die and who had helped bury him. Elizabeth believed the story and hired a man to find out what had become of her husband's money and property.

In the fall of 1817, Crockett explored the area of Shoal Creek, Tennessee, about eighty miles west of his home, during which he suffered another malarial attack. He liked the unsettled country enough to relocate there and moved his family to their new surroundings before any real system of law enforcement had

been established. At first there were no problems, since the settlers were law-abiding; however, after two years an unsavory element began to drift into the area, and the residents set up an
informal legal system to help keep order, appointing Crockett as
one of the area's magistrates. When a question of an unpaid debt
or a purloined pig came up, he would order a verbal warrant, and
his constable would bring the offender before him. Relying on
"principles of common justice and honesty between man and
man" and "natural born sense, and not on law," Magistrate
Crockett could get a reluctant debtor to make good without any
harsh penalties, but did hand out sentences of whipping for more
serious offenses such as theft.

Eventually the Shoal Creek settlement came under the control of Giles County, Tennessee, with most of the magistrates
and constables keeping their official status, and Crockett becoming justice of the peace with the added responsibility of issuing
written warrants. Since he had learned to write but still had some
difficulty with it, he colorfully described this added burden as "at
least a huckleberry over my persimmon." Luckily his constable,
more adept at reading and writing, helped to put the warrants
into legible form. The system worked within their limited authority, for, as he boasted, "My judgments were never appealed
from, and if they had been they would have stuck like wax." He
added, "I had never read a page in a law book in my life."

Crockett's entry into the political arena originated from a
certain touchiness when being toyed with, or made to look like
a bumpkin. Captain Matthews, one of the earlier settlers of the
region and a well-to-do farmer by frontier standards, informed
him that he planned to campaign for the rank of lieutenant
colonel of the local 57th Regiment of militia, and invited

Crockett to run with him for first major. Although Crockett had recently served as lieutenant with the Franklin County militia and had done his duty during the Creek War, he felt reluctant, believing by this time he had done his share of fighting and "wanted nothing to do with military appointments." Finally, after much insistence by Matthews, he agreed to run, and to attend a great "frolic" and cornhusking hosted by the captain to launch the campaign.

When he arrived at the festivities with Elizabeth and all of their assorted children, a friend took him aside and said that Matthews's son also sought the rank of major. Crockett interpreted this as a betrayal since Matthews would very likely shift his support to his son. Somewhat illogically, he saw the captain as "countenancing, if not encouraging a secret plan to beat me." The son probably decided to run for the post after Matthews had made the original invitation, but Crockett did not see it that way. When he asked for the truth, the older man admitted that young Matthews planned on running, and that he hated the idea of running against Crockett more than he would any other person in the county. This admission neither flattered nor mollified Crockett, who told the captain that his son had nothing to worry about since he had decided to run for the rank of lieutenant colonel instead of major. Matthews took the news with good humor and, in a sense of sportsmanship, led his new opponent back to the party and announced the development. Crockett made a short speech explaining the situation, concluding that, "as I had the whole family to run against any way, I was determined to levy on the head of the mess." The crowd loved it and Crockett emerged as the guileless innocent rising to the challenge. This perception paid off on election day, when he became the new lieutenant colonel of the 57th Regiment, with another candidate edging the younger Matthews out as major. He wore the title "colonel" proudly for the rest of his life.

He remained busy during 1818, farming, serving in his militia post, and as one of the town commissioners of Lawrenceburg, Tennessee, and, along with other commissioners worked on a variety of projects typical of a frontier town. They identified boundaries of land claims; helped select land for a proposed ironworks; made lists of taxable property; even took on custodianship of funds collected for the benefit of a child born out of wedlock. Crockett also compiled a census list, putting him in direct contact with future voters—and continued increasing his family when, on Christmas Day of that year, Elizabeth presented him with their first daughter, Rebecca Elvira.

His involvement in local affairs, success in the militia election, and his natural good humor led to his being approached to run for the Tennessee state legislature, representing Lawrence and Hickman counties. He resigned as town commissioner on January 1, 1821, officially threw his hat in the ring in February, but did not start his campaign immediately. On March 1, he left Tennessee with a drove of horses for an unidentified destination in southern North Carolina, perhaps planning to finance his election bid with money earned from sale of the animals. In what was reminiscent of his childhood ramblings, he took his time and spent three months on the trail, unconcerned with the election until he returned to Tennessee in early June. During the trip he stopped and visited with Mrs. Jacobs, a widow in east Tennessee from whose late husband he had borrowed a dollar ten years earlier. He had never forgotten the loan and although Mrs. Jacobs protested, he insisted she take the silver dollar.

For the campaign Crockett portrayed himself as an honest, uneducated frontiersman who knew very little about government. He admitted that he had "never read even a newspaper in my life, or any thing else on the subject," and "a public document I had never seen, nor did I know there was such things," but he caught on quickly. In Hickman County a controversy arose over moving the county seat from Vernon to one in a more centralized location. The candidate feigned bewilderment on how a whole town could be moved, but on the question itself he employed a valuable political posture and remained "non-committal."

Campaigning in the backwoods often consisted of two or more candidates hitting the trail together or meeting at a designated place where they could address an assemblage of potential voters. One of these occurred in Centerville, the town lobbying for the location of the county seat, with a party lasting for days, bringing together aspects of a squirrel hunt, barbecue, and dance, and marking Crockett's debut as a public speaker. Sides were drawn up for the squirrel hunt, with the one taking the fewest squirrels footing the bill for food and drink at the party. His side won, and at some point between the food and the dancing, it became his duty to formally address the voters. He fidgeted self-consciously, intimidated by the other candidate, and tried to beg off at the last minute since he knew his opponent "could speak prime, and I know'd too, that I wa'n't able to shuffle and cut with him." The other candidate, sensing and enjoying his opponent's discomfort, urged him on. Crockett opened his remarks by telling the crowd that "I had come for their votes, and if they didn't watch mighty close, I'd get them too," and admitting he could tell them nothing about the government, an admission that must have delighted his rival.

As the crowd watched wide-eyed and open-mouthed, the backwoodsman choked up, stammered, and fished about for something to say. Out of desperation he likened himself to a fellow who beat on the head of an empty barrel because he had heard there had been some cider in it a few days before, and now wanted to see if he could get any out. He stated that there had been "a little bit of a speech in me a while ago, but I believed I couldn't get it out." As the people roared in laughter, he threw in a couple of other anecdotes, and then quit while ahead. He also knew his audience enough to remark that he felt "as dry as a powder horn," and invited them over to the liquor stand to "wet our whistles a little."

His opponent found to his dismay that the vast majority of voters needed to get their whistles wet just as he took the stump. He explained governmental matters to a noticeably diminished audience while Crockett told a few stories, took a "horn," and generally back-slapped with the crowd at the bar, hitting on a formula that would serve him well during most of his political career.

The next stop on the campaign trail brought him to the town of Vernon, the center of the county seat controversy. When pressed for an opinion on this issue he did the unthinkable for a political candidate, admitting to the crowd that he did not know whether he thought moving the county seat to be right or not, and so he "couldn't promise either way."

On the following Monday a larger political meeting convened, bringing together the candidates for the governorship of Tennessee. These included William Carroll, the former soldier who had saved the day at Enotochopco, as well as candidates for Congress, and Crockett and his rival for the state legislature. He quaked inwardly at the thought of not only speaking in front of a large crowd, but also in front of "these big candidates," as he called them. Luckily, his turn came last and while the others spoke all day and generally wore down their audience, Crockett paid attention and absorbed as much as he could about governmental matters. When his turn came he faced the weary crowd, simply told one of his funny stories, and immediately won them over, feeling confident enough with their reaction to return home without stumping for additional votes in that area. The more serious political candidates may have thought he skirted the issues and merely acted the buffoon in his campaign, failing to realize that his backwoods constituents may have been no more familiar with the issues than he was. He succeeded in presenting to the voters an honest candidate with a good sense of humor, no better educated than they; in brief, one of their own. His formula worked, and in August 1821, he won the election by more than a two-to-one vote over his opponent, with Colonel Crockett becoming Representative Crockett of the Fourteenth Tennessee General Assembly. Besides winning the election that month, he became a father once again when Elizabeth gave birth to their daughter Matilda on August 2.

Later he liked to tell the story of his first meeting with another rising star in Tennessee politics, James Knox Polk. They met on their way to Murfreesboro, Tennessee, where the general assembly convened. Polk, a young, educated attorney from a well-to-do family, a future United States congressman and president, was traveling to Murfreesboro as clerk of the Tennessee State Senate. In a company of others, Polk addressed the fledgling representative with some amiable political chitchat.

"Well, Colonel, I suppose we shall have a radical change of the judiciary at the next session of the legislature," Polk said. Crockett answered, "Very likely, sir," and then detached himself from the conversation as quickly as possible, fearing that someone would ask him what the judiciary actually was. "If I knowed I wish I may be shot," he said, "I don't indeed believe I had ever before heard that there was any such thing in all nature."

His career as a legislator began on September 17, 1821, with his assignment to the Committee of Propositions and Grievances. Despite his professed ignorance of government, he pitched in, always championing his constituents, the poor landholders and squatters of west Tennessee, the major focus for the whole of his political life.

The land from which the state of Tennessee was created had been the western part of North Carolina until the federal government acquired the territory in 1789. In ceding this vast territory, North Carolina greatly reduced the amount of land entitled to its citizens for their Revolutionary War service. The state only agreed to the transaction under the condition that lands in the newly formed Tennessee remain available to reimburse the North Carolinian soldiers. The government decided that lands in eastern Tennessee would be used to satisfy its obligation to the veterans, but when this land proved insufficient to fulfill all the warrants, Congress agreed to open land in the western portion of the state. This gave the warrant holders preference and put pioneers and frontiersmen, who had run the risks in settling the land, in danger of being moved off the parcels they had developed. Crockett fought tenaciously against this possibility, in addition to voting to excuse landholders in west

Tennessee from paying double taxes as a penalty for being delinquent in their payments. In his first session he also sided with William Carroll in the legislature's vote for governor, finally took a stand on the issue of whether the county seat should be in Vernon or Centerville (he supported Vernon, but the legislature awarded Centerville the seat), and generally supported any measures that would keep poor farmers and settlers from being uprooted.

Trouble at home interrupted before he could settle into the business of state politics. He and Elizabeth had invested her nest egg and the money from their land sales on an idea of his. He built a dam, grist and powder mills, and a distillery on Shoal Creek, which were just getting into operation, with Elizabeth in charge, when Crockett left for Murfreesboro. They had hoped for a steady income by keeping their neighbors supplied with the frontier basics of flour, gunpowder, and whiskey, but had not anticipated the heavy rains that flooded the Tennessee River and Shoal Creek, and the flash flood that wiped out everything save part of the dam. When the devastating news reached him on September 29, he secured a leave of absence, rushed home, and found that nothing could be salvaged. The disaster left the Crockett family broke and in debt for the cost of constructing the dam and mills, but he feared these matters less than Elizabeth's wrath. Although they had gone in on the plan together, he felt responsible for the loss. To his relief, she did not berate him but merely advised him to pay their debts as soon as he could. He agreed, writing later that it was "better to keep a good conscience with an empty purse, than to get a bad opinion of myself, with a full one."

He returned to the legislature in October, continuing to work for the interests of the west Tennessee squatters, and becoming increasingly aware of the growing tension and class distinction between the poorer, western section of the state, the politically powerful center, and the more affluent east. Occasionally these distinctions were demonstrated on the floor of the general assembly, as in the case of an incident in the early days of the first session when the roughly dressed representative from Lawrence and Hickman counties rose to speak on an issue before the floor. Following him, the better-educated and more fashionably dressed James C. Mitchell, representing Rhea, Hamilton, and McMinn counties, took an opposing stand and made the mistake of calling Crockett the "gentleman from the cane"—referring to the dense canebrakes in the unsettled region the gentleman represented. Nervous laughter rippled through the assembly. To the novice lawmaker, still ill at ease and sensitive about his image as a backwoodsmen among refined men, this amounted to a humiliating insult. He accosted Mitchell afterward and demanded an apology with the threat of a fight as the only alternative. Mitchell refused to be drawn in, calmly stating that he meant no insult by the remark, and intended nothing more than a descriptive reference to the area Crockett represented. The dismissive explanation did not satisfy the gentleman from the cane but the two avoided violence.

At the next meeting of the assembly, Crockett followed Mitchell in his address to the floor. Since their last encounter he had managed to obtain a cambric ruffle, a decorative piece worn on the front of gentlemen's dress shirts of the time. When he rose to speak he did so with the ruffle pinned to the front of his coarse, homespun shirt. The incongruous sight had the desired effect on the members of the legislature, who broke into prolonged laughter, with Mitchell proving more sensitive and touchy than his colleague as he retreated from the chamber in exasperation.

When the legislature adjourned on November 17, 1821, Representative Crockett returned home but did not linger, setting out on an expedition to explore the Obion River country of Tennessee, 150 miles northwest of his farm. The collapse of his mill enterprise, the increasing pressure from creditors, and the desire to better provide for his growing family prompted his search for new and richer land. His oldest son, John Wesley, and another young man joined him on his journey west, during which he found the land he sought. Severe earthquakes some years earlier had left the country a broken tangle of crevices and dead-fall trees, the perfect environment for wild game, especially bears. He found a spot that appealed to him, with the nearest house seven miles on the opposite side of the Obion River. Hobbling their horses in an open field to graze, the explorers set out on foot to call on the neighbor, undeterred by the need to cross the river and the heavily flooded adjoining countryside in winter weather. They waded along for miles with the water at times up to their necks, with young John Wesley swimming beside them. Crockett probed ahead of the others with a pole, looking for deep pockets, sometimes chopping down trees and branches for makeshift bridges.

At last they reached their destination and were welcomed by their surprised host, who brought out his jug for the men while his wife tended to the wet and shivering boy. "If a horn wasn't good then, there was no use for its invention," Crockett remembered later, even allowing his son to take part. They stayed the night, alternately warming themselves between the fire and the jug until he admitted that he had taken enough to "drive out all the cold that was in me, and about three times as much more."

A team of boatmen, who had taken their small craft farther up the Obion then anyone had gone before, also stayed at the house. They carried a load of whiskey, flour, salt, sugar, and molded metal castings, but the falling river waters and the inability to get past a tangle of dead-fall trees had left them stranded. While they waited for heavy rains to bring up the river level, the men agreed to accompany Crockett back to his land claim and assist him in constructing a small cabin. In return, and in exchange for four barrels of meal, a barrel of salt, and ten gallons of whiskey, he agreed to serve as a hunter on their intended voyage a hundred miles farther up the Obion River, leaving John Wesley and the other young man behind at the cabin with a supply of bacon on hand plus the venison from a deer he had killed.

As the boat crew waited for the river to rise, their new hunter ranged over the countryside all day in search of game, killing one deer and five good-size elk by nightfall. He hung the game in trees along the river, intending to recover it by light of day as the boat came through, without knowing that the craft had cleared the downed trees and had traveled two miles beyond him. He located the traders by firing his gun, yelling into the darkness, and finally wading into the icy waters again. Meantime, some of the crew had set out in a skiff and found their hunter cut up by thorns and briers, hungry, cold, and, he said, "so tired that I could hardly work my jaws to eat." Luckily he could still drink, and another lifesaving draft of whiskey brought him around once they hauled him back to the main boat.

In the morning they collected only four of the six animals Crockett had shot, enough to leave the boatmen well supplied as they proceeded up the river. With the loan of their skiff and one of the young crew members, he returned to his newly found acreage, where he worked with his son, the young man with them, and the borrowed boatman to clear a field and plant a crop of corn. When he had stocked enough deer and bear meat to sustain his hired hands, he and his son returned to Lawrence to collect the rest of the family.

Upon his arrival home in the spring he found a recall letter awaiting him, directing him to return to Murfreesboro by July 22 for a special session of the legislature. During this session, which lasted until August 24, Crockett continued his support of the settlers on west Tennessee land with renewed vigor since he could now count himself as one of them. He also supported a bill allowing Tennessee to disperse vacant land north and east of the Congressional Line, an arbitrary boundary that sepa-rated the state into eastern and western sections. The bill, in-tended to finance statewide education, failed. Among the other measures he endorsed were funds for an ironworks, the preven-tion of fraud in the execution of last wills and testaments, relief for widows and orphans, and a bill "for the relief of Mathias, a free man of color." He was successful in opposing a bill that would restore certain fees to justices of the peace and consta-bles. Under this system, rife with corruption, unscrupulous peace officers urged people to file civil cases, from which the officials would collect a percentage of the settlement.

Crockett settled his debts at home with the sale of 160 acres of land on Shoal Creek, three miles east of Lawrenceburg; then, in 1822, he gathered his family and moved them to their new homestead in the wilds of the Obion River country. He spent the fall harvesting his corn crop, hunting, and delighting in the abundance of game in this new area, especially the dangerous black bear. Just before Christmas one of the problems of living far from the edge of civilization caught up with him: he ran out of gunpowder. He could have gone to Jackson, the county seat of Madison County, forty miles away, for a new supply, but heavy rains had once again turned the Obion country into an inland sea. Luckily, one of Elizabeth's brothers had recently moved a scant six miles from them on the opposite side of the river, and was in possession of a keg of powder. Crockett needed it to keep his family sustained with meat during the winter, but he also wanted to be able to fire off "Christmas-guns," probably the only Yuletide festivities the Crockett children could count on. Over his wife's protestation he determined that he would walk, or more accurately wade, to her brother's house for the powder. She told him of her certainty that he would either freeze to death or be drowned, but he "didn't believe half of this" and set off with four inches of snow on the ground, armed only with his rifle, tomahawk, knife, and some dry clothes tied in a bundle. He waded through the freezing, flooded countryside, crossed the river on submerged logs, fell in up to his chin, and only kept his rifle and spare clothes dry by carrying them over his head. After dragging himself from the river, numb with cold, he changed his clothing, managed to trudge the last five miles and stagger into his brother-in-law's house by nightfall, half dead from hypothermia. He remained there two nights, helping to lay in a supply of venison before leaving with his gunpowder. By then, the falling temperature had coated the river with ice, but not to a thickness that would sustain his weight, and halfway across he plunged through. Luckily, he had left his rifle on the far bank while he carried the keg. He lost neither, but did have to subject himself to the freezing water twice to bring everything across.

After recovering his strength, he shouldered the powder keg, and in plunging toward home saw that a path had been broken through the ice on the flooded land and concluded that it could only have been made by a bear. With shaking hands he primed his rifle and followed the path—right to his cabin door. The trail had actually been cut by one of the young men who lived with them and who had gone out at Elizabeth's request in search of her husband. Crockett stumbled into the cabin, once again returning from the dead, later admitting that he did not know "how much any body could suffer and not die." He added, "When I got home I wasn't quite dead, but mighty nigh it; but I had my powder, and that was what I went for."

His powder quest paid off the next morning in a freezing sleet when he went out after game. He had already brought down two turkeys when his hunting dogs went berserk, leading him to the biggest black bear he had ever seen. He took off in pursuit and managed to put two balls into the animal with little effect, and at one point closing in with knife and tomahawk when the beast latched on to one of his dogs. He quickly abandoned the idea of hand-to-claw combat, realizing that the bear "would hug me altogether too close for comfort," if it caught him. The battle ended when he retrieved his rifle, and brought the animal down with a third shot. The bear, which he estimated to weigh over six hundred pounds, along with other game, kept his family supplied with meat for the rest of a long, cold winter.

By February 1823, Crockett had accumulated enough animal skins to trade to make a trip to the county seat at Jackson with his son John Wesley. There they loaded up on sugar, salt, coffee, gunpowder, and lead, and were about to return home when he decided to have a drink or two with some fellow soldiers from the Creek War he had met. In the course of their reunion, the veterans mingled with a gathering of local officials, including Dr. William E. Butler, the town commissioner of Jackson and nephew-in-law of Andrew Jackson; and Duncan McIver and Major Joseph Lynn, members of Madison County's court of pleas and quarters—all candidates for the Tennessee legislature. The subject of Crockett's recent term in the general assembly came up with someone jokingly suggesting that he run again. Although he had enjoyed his roll as a state representative, he shrugged off the idea since he lived forty miles from the nearest white settlement, Jackson, and 150 miles from Murfreesboro. He assured them that he wanted no part of being a candidate and headed home with his son and goods.

Two weeks later a neighbor stopped by his cabin and congratulated him on his candidacy for the legislature. When Crockett expressed confusion the man produced a copy of the *Jackson Pioneer* that identified him as a state house hopeful. While the article may have been nothing more than a mistake on the part of a newspaperman seeing him with the candidates in Jackson, or overhearing part of their conversation, Crockett saw it otherwise. He explained to the exasperated Elizabeth that the article had ridiculed him and that someone had to be held accountable. He decided that he *would* run again and make those he thought were lampooning him eat their words by winning the election. He hired a man to work his farm while he again took to the campaign trail, capitalizing on his image as the "gentleman from the cane" and a great bear hunter. As word of his candidacy and popularity spread, the other candidates became concerned, and in a March caucus decided that the best strategy for defeating him required them to rally around a single candidate. Dr. Butler, the most talented of the three, and with the greatest chance of winning, received the endorsement of the other two.

Facing this strong adversary, Crockett determined to "push ahead and go through," and took advantage of a political meeting arranged for Colonel Adam Alexander, a candidate for the United States Congress. The rally progressed to the point where Alexander "treated" the crowd, a common practice of campaigning politicians of buying alcoholic refreshments for potential voters. Crockett attended and besides taking a horn or two, benefited by Alexander taking him around and introducing him as a candidate for the state legislature. Butler, also in attendance, recognized his opponent and hailed him—"Damn it, Crockett, is that you?" the doctor asked. The bear hunter answered, "Be sure it is, but I don't want it understood that I have come electioneering. I have crept out of the cane, to see what discoveries I could make among the white folk." Once he had the crowd's attention he went on to explain how he planned to have a special campaigning buckskin shirt made with extra large pockets that would hold a large twist of tobacco and a bottle of liquor. Then when a man spit out his quid to take an offered drink, the candidate could replace the "chaw" without leaving the voter any worse off than when he found him. He emphasized the poverty he had in common with most of the voters by explaining how all of his children and even his hunting dogs would pitch in, gathering raccoon pelts and wolf scalps to help finance his campaign. The crowd enjoyed the performance, including Butler, who good-naturedly admitted that he could not match his opponent in campaign methods, prompting Crockett to reply with a bit of an edge that he would give him better evidence of that come election time in August.

Butler had some clear advantages in the race. He was better off financially, had a better grasp of the issues, and the skill to explain them at public gatherings. Crockett countered by turning his opponent's strengths against him. After enjoying the hospitality of Butler's home, a courtesy extended to candidates on the campaign trail together, he told backwoods voters that Butler walked on fancier material in his carpets than their own wives wore as clothing. While campaigning together, he made sure he paid close attention to Butler's speech—the one speech he gave at every gathering—until he had committed it to memory. When an opportunity arose in which Crockett addressed the crowd first, he delivered Butler's speech word for word, leaving the doctor dumbfounded and fumbling for something to say. The clowning and the antics worked. Crockett won the election by a margin of 247 votes and returned to Murfreesboro in September 1823 as the representative in the Fifteenth General Assembly of Carroll, Henderson, Humphreys, Madison, and Perry counties of western Tennessee.

He served through 1824, championing the rights of the poor as he had done before, and sitting on several committees, including the Select Committee on Military Affairs, in acknowledgment of his service in the Creek War as well as of being an officer of militia. He felt more comfortable in the role of legislator now, turning his persona as the backwoods bumpkin on and off as needed. He took particular pride in one episode during this term in which, by showing that he owed no allegiance to anyone other than his west Tennessee constituents, he proved that he would not "forsake principle for party, or for the purpose of following after big men."

Tennessee's senator John Williams's term had expired and he sought reelection, to the chagrin of his bitter opponent Andrew Jackson, who had emerged as a power in the state's political machine. Even though preparing to run for president, Jackson agreed to run against Williams for senator, as the only man renowned enough to defeat him. In 1824, senators were chosen by state lawmakers, and Jackson barely won the legislature's decision, then resigned the post, having effectively prevented Williams's return to Washington. Crockett became a vocal supporter of Williams during the race because he believed in the senator's honesty and devotion, and made it clear that he had voted against "Old Hickory," stating, "It was the best vote I ever gave." He had just defeated the nephew-in-law of the state's political strongman in an election, and now had publicly voted against the man himself, causing Jackson to take renewed interest in his former sergeant.

Since adjournment of the Tennessee assembly on October 22, 1824, marked the end of Crockett's career as a state legislator, he immediately looked toward a higher office, that of representative from Tennessee to the United States Congress. The incumbent congressman, Colonel Adam Alexander, also the surveyor general of the Tenth Surveyor District in western Tennessee, presented a tough opposition. Financially secure, experienced, and with influence in the local press, his only exploitable fault proved to be his support of a tariff law in 1824 that benefited manufacturers but few of his constituents. Crockett toyed with the idea of challenging Alexander but professed a reluctance to commit to the race, stating, "It was a step above my knowledge, and I know'd nothing about Congress matters." Even so, urged on by his supporters, he decided to take up the challenge in 1825 but found that his old backwoods, down-home humor would not sustain him. He could not compete with Alexander's expensive "treating" stops and lost the election by 267 votes, admitting that his opponent "made a mash of me."

Rebirth and Baptism

As an unemployed politician Crockett needed something to occupy his time and sustain his family. His newest venture, another gamble on a business with which he had no experience, involved the shipping of barrel staves down the Mississippi River for sale in New Orleans. He hired some hands to cut the staves while others constructed two flatboats on Obion Lake, twenty-five miles west of his home, and worked with them until the onset of autumn, when he had to lay in a food supply for his family. He embarked on a hunt for bears fattened for hibernation and soon had enough meat salted down for the winter. Hunting proved more attractive to him than cutting barrel staves, so with little guilt he accommodated any neighbor who needed his considerable skills to help bring in game, returning only once to his labors with the boats and staves. With one or more companions, sometimes with one of his sons, and accompanied by eight large hunting dogs, he exacted a terrible slaughter of the bear population of west Tennessee. On one occasion he found a stranger grubbing for food in the woods to feed his family, took him under his wing, and taught him how to bring down a bear, leaving the man with over a thousand pounds of meat by the time he finished the instruction.

Crockett's passion for the hunt entailed more than just standing back and firing his rifle at a bear his hounds had treed. On one occasion he followed the dogs in a pursuit that continued beyond sunset, through icy creeks, tangled underbrush, and up and down heavily wooded hills. Eventually, he managed to get two shots off when his prey took to a tree, but he could not determine if he had hit his mark in the darkness. As he loaded his rifle for a third shot the bear tumbled out of the tree into the midst of his dogs and joined battle, the fight raging around Crockett until the animals fell into an earthquake crevice. In the darkness he got off another shot at close range, doing little damage, and finally finished the beast off by descending into the crevice, feeling along the bear's shoulder while it still battled the dogs, and plunging his butcher knife into its heart. While not all of his hunts were as harrowing as this one, they were all bountiful. He estimated that during that fall and winter, and one month into the spring of 1826, he and his hunting companions killed a total of 105 bears.

With the hunting season over, he returned to his barrel staves enterprise. After his men had completed the flatboats and loaded them with thirty thousand staves, he confidently set off down the Obion River with cargo and crew. Only when they reached the rough currents of the wide Mississippi did he realize that his pilot knew no more about navigating the demanding river than he did. Besides that, the crew became panicky. At one point they came alongside some experienced Ohio boatmen who urged them to continue down the river all night since they were unable to land, and in an effort to keep the boats together, Crockett ordered them lashed to each other. This made the boats more unwieldy, and people on shore ran to the riverbanks with lanterns, shouting instructions to them as they careened along sideways in the current. The exhausted and disheartened amateur skipper gave up trying to reach shore, went into the cabin of the aft boat to warm himself by the fire, and lamented the fact that he was not bear hunting at the moment. Just when it seemed the situation could get no worse, the hatch of the cabin suddenly crashed down, closing off the only exit. As the crew scrambled frantically on deck the ungainly boats slammed into a tangle of submerged trees at the head of an island just above Memphis and began to founder. Crockett tried to escape through the hatchway but a cascade of water forced him back. His only escape route, a hole in the side of the cabin, was not quite large enough for him to pull himself through, so with both arms thrust out of the opening he yelled to his crew, "Pull my arms off, or force me through!" He described the situation as "neck or nothing, come out or sink."

Pull they did, dragging him through the narrow hole and skinning off all of his clothing in the process. The boats, the staves, and the crew's possessions were lost, but all survived, spending the night on the driftwood trees about a mile from either shore. Despite yet another disastrous business loss and the fact that he sat naked in the middle of the Mississippi River, Crockett felt "happier and better off than I ever had in my life." He had again cheated death.

In the morning a boat came up the river from Memphis, plucked the shivering Tennesseans from the island, and brought

them to town. A crowd had gathered to watch the rescue, among
them Major Marcus B. Winchester, a local dry-goods merchant,
who philanthropically provided the hapless boatmen with clothing and a little money. The merchant's generosity impressed
Crockett, who would later say he was a friend "I never can forget
as long as I am able to go ahead at any thing." Before leaving the
Mississippi, Crockett and one of his young crewmen took passage on a boat downriver to see if their own boats had resurfaced,
and if so, were salvageable. One of the boats, they were told, had
been seen fifty miles below the wreck, but despite some efforts
could not be brought to shore.

With his river-faring adventures at an end he headed east,
looking ahead to the safety and familiarity of bear hunting and
another run for Congress the next year. In the spring of 1826
he arrived home to more debts incurred by his latest debacle.
His finances were in such disarray that some creditors were
moved by pity, as in the case of one man who had been trying
to evict him from a piece of leased land and then decided not to
follow through after all. Crockett spent the summer months on
"juries of view," whose job it was to blaze trails for new roads
with the assistance of neighbors along the way.

In early 1827 his benefactor, Marcus Winchester, invited him
to return to Memphis, loaned him money, and began speaking
on his behalf in his run for the Twentieth Congress. He gratefully accepted the help since his opponents were again the formi-
dable incumbent, Colonel Adam Alexander, whom he called "my
friend Aleck," and General William Arnold, the major-general
of Tennessee's western district militia. The Winchester loan en-
abled Crockett to campaign with new energy, paying for travel,
printed materials, and the inevitable "treating." He also enjoyed

the benefit of his old electioneering style of warming up the voters with some humor, identifying himself with them through the use of down-home expressions, and exploiting the stuffiness of his opponents. In this the other candidates played into his hands, haranguing the crowds with long speeches, fighting over obscure issues, and generally ignoring Crockett as a serious threat while he mixed with voters as one of their own.

On one occasion he spoke first and briefly at a campaign stop, following his belief that "a short horse is soon curried." Alexander spoke next and then Arnold, who replied to Alexander point for point, without so much as acknowledging Crockett. The tedium was only broken by the clucking of a flock of guinea fowls that appeared on the scene. The flustered Arnold directed that the flock be driven off, after which he completed his lengthy address. Afterward Crockett commended him on being able to understand the language of fowls. The general, he said, not only lacked the courtesy to acknowledge him as a candidate, but when his friends the guinea fowls appeared chattering, "Crockett, Crockett, Crockett," Arnold had them driven off. The crowd delighted in this bit of nonsense, but it did not please Arnold.

In the election in August, aided by a hundred-dollar loan and the flock of guinea fowls, Crockett achieved his goal of becoming Tennessee's newest congressman in the United States House of Representatives.

Congressman Crockett

efore setting off for Washington, Crockett took time off with Elizabeth to visit his wife's family in Swannanoa, North Carolina. He brought John Wesley along to accompany Elizabeth back home while he proceeded to Congress afterward, leaving the younger children with relatives in west Tennessee. They left their home on October 1, and the trip proved to be a torture for him when his malaria flared up again in the middle of the month. They managed to reach her family's home, but he shivered in sickness for weeks. He recovered long enough to witness a duel on November 6 between his friend Samuel P. Carson and a man named Robert B. Vance, a challenge that grew from insults hurled while they campaigned against each other in the North Carolina congressional race. Carson prevailed in the violent encounter and Crockett galloped back to the duelist's home announcing, "The victory is ours!" Vance died the next day.

He left Elizabeth and his son in Swannanoa to return to west

Tennessee on their own while he set off, shakily, in the company of the duel victor, Carson. The trip became an ordeal since he had not fully recovered from the malarial fever and the debilitating effects of bloodletting by physicians. "I have thought that I was never to see my family any more," he later wrote.

In Washington the weakened new congressman took lodging and recuperated at Mrs. Ball's boardinghouse, an establishment accommodating a number of legislators and other government officials. He needed all the strength he could muster since he intended to push through the House his land bill on behalf of the squatters of west Tennessee. In his naivete he may have believed this would be an easy task but either did not recognize or chose to ignore the very real progression toward partisan politics in the country. He determined to stay above enforced loyalties, remaining his own man, and answering only to his constituents and to his conscience.

Andrew Jackson's political rival, Secretary of State Henry Clay of Kentucky, opposed Jackson as he prepared for a run at the presidency. Crockett tested his political independence in these dangerous waters immediately after his own election. While passing through Nashville he called on Clay's son-in-law, James Erwin, seeking an introduction to the eminent Kentuckian, going so far as to ask advice from Clay, through Erwin, on voting for the Speaker of the House of Representatives. Erwin fired off a letter to Clay that amounted to an intelligence report on the meeting, describing his visitor as a rough, uncouth, loud talker, but also "independent and fearless and has a popularity at home that is unaccountable." Clay could not have ignored the assessment of Crockett as "the only man that I now know in Tennessee that could openly oppose Genl. Jackson in his own district and be elected to congress." Crockett had not abandoned his old general at this point, nor had he any intention of opposing him. He continued to speak and write about Jackson in glowing terms, likening him to a diamond in the rough and predicting that he would be the next president.

Crockett launched into his land bill campaign within three days of the beginning of the congressional session. The land question in Tennessee involved the state requesting from the federal government all pieces of public land on both sides of its east–west dividing line. Tennessee would then sell parcels of land to the highest bidders and use the money for public education. While Crockett originally supported this idea, his greatest concern remained the squatters who occupied the lands and were in danger of being dispossessed and uprooted if the plan succeeded. He wanted the land made available at prices reasonable enough for the people who actually lived on it to be able to buy it, admonishing his colleagues, "We should at least occasionally legislate for the poor." He remained optimistic about the passage of his bill even though the issue had little interest outside west Tennessee, and became less interested in anything else that transpired on the floor of the House. The windy speeches he heard seemed to accomplish nothing so he absented himself when the sessions did not concern him or his sector of Tennessee. In addition to his waning interest in the dull routine of the House, his malarial fever returned a number of times and he missed still more days. By the time Congress adjourned in May 1828, the land bill had been tabled, over the objection of the Tennessee delegation, with no hope of anything being done with it until early 1829.

Crockett drifted home when he felt strong enough to travel,

spent the rest of the summer constructing another grist mill, and struggled with his ever-increasing debts. During the summer Andrew Jackson defeated John Quincy Adams in the national election and became the seventh president of the United States. Crockett, still a loyal Tennessean, predicted that the new president would "shine conspicuous."

The champion of squatters' rights returned when Congress reconvened on December 1, 1828. A month later he proposed an amendment to the Tennessee land bill of the previous year, in which the land would be given directly to the people who had been living on it and improving it, thus bypassing the provision calling for the profits to go to the state for education. This stance brought him into conflict with James K. Polk and the others of the Tennessee delegation, as well as President Jackson. Crockett reasoned that the state wanted some of the funds from vacant lands, most of which were located in his district, used for education, but that his constituents would not benefit from the schools. He explained that he answered to higher authorities than his colleagues, his state, or his president—those being the people who put him in office. "The children of my people never saw the inside of a college in their lives, and never are likely to do so," he said. Polk and the other Tennessee delegates tried to warn him off this course, but were unaccustomed to Crockett's stubbornness as he forged ahead without any sense of political compromise or the alienation of his colleagues.

The political forces in the country continued to polarize—the Democrats under Jackson and the National Republicans under Clay, with the Republicans and anti-Jackson Democrats eventually coalescing into the Whig party. Crockett maintained his professed independence from any party, but as he began to evolve as a frontier "character" in national newspapers, he emerged as a potential asset to Whigs and a liability to Democrats. One such incident occurred in 1828, involving his appearance at a small dinner party at the White House with then president John Quincy Adams and a number of prominent Whigs. Soon after, a description of the event appeared in a Whig newspaper, which portrayed Crockett as an uncouth, apish boor who drank from finger bowls, used all the cups attached to a punch bowl, and accused a servant of stealing his food when he removed his plate. When Crockett heard the story he was furious, since the description of his behavior was utter fiction. He appealed to two of the other dinner guests to attest to his good conduct, which they did in an open letter to the same newspaper.

As he distanced himself from the Tennessee Democrats, Crockett drifted closer to the Whigs. He lived with some Whig party members at Mrs. Ball's rooming house and dined with them at the executive mansion; they defended him in the press, counseled him in the halls of Congress, and helped with his speeches. While he continued to push for his version of his all-important land bill, he ignored the Tennessee delegates who even offered to alter the bill so that the squatters would get first opportunity to buy the land. He refused to budge, however, outraging Polk and the others when he publicly criticized them and questioned their motives. He became so obsessed with getting his version of the bill passed that he offered to support anything other members of Congress asked in exchange for their votes. Even in the give-and-take bargaining and compromise of national politics, this blatant bartering for votes on the floor of the House seemed an embarrassing breach of decorum.

Crockett could not get his bill passed but he did manage to have Polk's version delayed, and Congress tabled the matter in January 1829. He returned home in the spring to the prospect of a tough campaign if he hoped to retain his seat in the Twenty-first Congress. He had little to offer the voters, having failed to get his land bill passed, but did manage to get a new postal route established in his west Tennessee district.

The pressures of campaigning were heightened by the gloomy news that the rest of his state's delegation, led by James K. Polk, were determined to see him defeated. He launched into his campaign vigorously even though he faced a new type of opponent in the form of Tennessee's political machine. In the past he had gotten by with his charismatic personality and a bit of ironic humor to turn the tables on a straight-laced or stuffy rival. This time the opposition brought the fight to him, lampooning him in the press, falsifying letters to editors in support of Polk's version of the land bill, and generally labeling Crockett a traitor to Tennessee. One candidate even attacked him on moral grounds, citing drunkenness and adultery. Every accusation Crockett countered with worse charges—ones he fabricated. Finally, his opponent assembled an array of witnesses to fight the false statements and publicly humiliate him as a liar, but Crockett had caught on to the plan, and at their next appearance he made the usual false charges, then stunned his audience by freely admitting he had been lying before his adversary could present his witnesses. He told the onlookers that he had lied to answer the lies leveled against him. Both candidates had been lying, he said, but only one freely admitted it. Once again he became the hero of the crowd, and his opponent, unable to handle the illogic of it all, withdrew from the race.

The task of unseating Crockett fell to Colonel Adam Alexander, who had defeated him in his initial run for Congress in 1825. Now, however, the game had changed. If the incumbent did not have much to show his constituents for his first term, at least he projected the image of a man who still intended to plug away on their behalf. The voters responded by returning him to Congress with a resounding 6,773 votes to Alexander's 3,641. It must have been of special satisfaction to Crockett to learn that one of the other incumbents from Polk's camp failed to get reelected and another barely squeaked by. Polk himself returned to Congress.

Crockett plunged back into his fight for the land bill when the House convened in December 1829, but without making progress. Finally, he agreed to compromise on some of his points, giving up his idea that the land be given to those who already lived on it. He settled for a proposal that the land be sold at twelve and a half cents per acre, with the squatters occupying the land given first opportunity to buy. Debate dragged on throughout the spring of 1830, but the bill met defeat in May. In a last-ditch effort, Crockett offered to revise the terms of the squatters' right to the land to keep the bill alive but succeeded only in getting his motion tabled until the next session. With all of the bickering he became more frustrated with the resistance of the rest of the Tennessee delegation. He could not conceive of elected officials opposing anything immediately beneficial to the people they represented.

As he slid further from the Democrats and into the arms of the Whigs, Crockett became more of an embarrassment to Andrew Jackson. Although he never stood directly opposed to Jackson, he did so against Polk's clique of delegates, all of whom were clearly in the president's camp. He continued to profess his love and admiration for his former general, but also saw the importance of declaring his independence of him, and began to develop catchphrases that stated his position. In justifying his career-damaging course on the land bill in opposition to his state's delegates and, of course, the president, he declared that he would rather be "politically dead than hypocritically immortalized." In response to accusations that he had abandoned Jackson and thus become a traitor to his state, he took the position that he remained "a Jackson man but General Jackson is not." He pledged to continue to follow his conscience and never wear a collar identifying him as a dog belonging to the chief executive.

Crockett and Jackson began gravitating to opposite poles of every issue. When a bill came before the House to build a national road from Washington to New Orleans, Crockett proposed an amendment to have the road pass through Memphis, arguing that no road could compete with the Mississippi River anyway. The House rejected his amendment as well as the original bill. When another piece of legislation proposed a road to Maysville, Kentucky, he spoke out against it but then voted for it. He later justified his reversal by explaining to his constituents in Tennessee that they would have benefited since the road eventually would have been continued to Memphis. The House passed this bill but Jackson vetoed it. When Congress voted to override the veto, Crockett supported the override.

He opposed the tariff that financed such government projects as road building as a method of squeezing money from the poor. He argued for the abolition of the military academy at West Point since it seemed to him just another waste of tax money, offering opportunity only to the sons of the rich. He remained a volunteer soldier at heart, blind to the need of the United States to have a professionally trained officers' corps for its small standing army. The memory lingered of the slight he suffered during the Creek War when his superior took action on the word of an officer but ignored his.

The major rift with Jackson occurred over the Indian Removal Bill, which the president himself introduced in early 1830. The legislation called for the uprooting of peaceful Indians from their tribal lands in the Southeast to reservations west of the Mississippi. For the first time Crockett opposed a measure benefiting his constituents. With the Indians' removal, the western Tennessee squatters would have more land available to them and would no longer worry about living so close to a culture and people they did not trust. But Crockett opposed the bill, not only because Jackson favored it but because Jackson would be given a half million dollars, with no regulation of the money, to implement it. More important, the gentleman from the cane could not overlook the moral issue: moving a whole population of native people from their ancestral homes.

The debates on the issue dragged on for months with Crockett remaining uncharacteristically quiet. In May the bill finally passed by a margin of five votes, with his, alone among the Tennessee delegation's, cast against it.

In the midst of the battle over Indian removal the rebel congressman opposed yet another measure backed by Jackson, a bill to award the widow of naval hero Stephen Decatur the sum of $100,000. He had nothing against Mrs. Decatur, whose husband had been killed in a duel in 1820, but argued that Congress had no authority to use taxpayers' money for a private charitable act, even one as noble as this. He also pointed out that every veteran's widow would be entitled to such a benefit, something he knew Congress would never authorize. His arguments helped to defeat the bill. Afterward he offered to contribute to a private collection on the widow's behalf.

While he continued to insist that he remained a Jackson man, despite the president's drift from a moral and ethical course, in fact they were bitter opponents, something that enhanced his reputation as an independent and increased his image in the press as a genuine frontier character, but could not guarantee him his seat in the House.

He faced a tough fight during the summer of 1831 in his campaign for reelection. Not only did he have a problem in the eyes of the people of his district in opposing the Indian removal bill, but also had the Polk clique actively working against him, again attacking him as a traitor to Jackson and Tennessee. Newspapers printed his record of missed votes on the floor of the House, without offering a comparison of the absenteeism of other representatives. Jacksonian Democrats ridiculed him in the press as the "Whig jester," and his reputation as a frontier bumpkin. His opponents, whom he referred to as "little four-pence-ha'-penny limbs of law," advertised public appearances for him of which he had no knowledge. When he failed to appear, the disappointed crowd listened to Jackson men attack the Tennessean's record.

He constantly campaigned on the defensive, being assailed wherever he spoke by what he called "every little pin-hook lawyer," and being "hunted down like a wild varment" by every newspaper. In the 1831 campaign race he faced William Fitzgerald, a Weakley County attorney whom Crockett described as "a little county court lawyer with very little standing," and "a perfect lick spittle."

The rigors of the campaign wore him down. He lost his easy-going ways and good humor. When Fitzgerald made some scurrilous accusations against him, he threatened to thrash his opponent frontier-style if they were repeated. When the time of confrontation came, Fitzgerald leveled the same accusations and Crockett started after him. As he approached, the lawyer produced a hidden gun and pointed it at the chest of his unarmed opponent, forcing him to resume his seat.

Even Jackson entered the fray, urging friends in Madison County not to disgrace themselves by reelecting "that profligate man." In the end Madison County proved his undoing, costing him the election by 586 votes. Crockett consoled himself with the thought that he preferred to be "beaten and be a man than to be elected and be a little puppy dog."

The Lion of the West

After the election Crockett returned to his home for a long period of isolation and reevaluation, later writing that the people of his district were induced to "take a stay on me" for the Twenty-second Congress, due to the tricks of his opponents. He continued to console himself that he had followed his conscience and tried to do what he considered right in the interests of "the common man." In early 1831 he began to use the expression "Be always sure you're right then go ahead," which became the motto forever associated with David Crockett of Tennessee.

During this period as an out-of-work congressman, he farmed, hunted, and borrowed money to contend with his debts and to build a war chest for his next campaign. The Bank of the United States, a Whig stronghold, proved particularly generous, later even canceling the debt he owed. He may not have realized that accepting such generosity could place him in another form of indebtedness.

It was frustrating for him to be so far from the seat of power in the capitol, where he had developed a dual persona that he enjoyed and used to its fullest advantage. In Washington he behaved as a respectable congressman but enjoyed the attention he received as a rough, far-west backwoodsman. In west Tennessee he remained a trustworthy and reliable frontier neighbor, but enjoyed the status of his congressional title. Some years before, he had ridden up to a friend's cornshucking dressed as if on the floor of Congress, then rolled up his sleeves and joined the work as an ordinary neighbor. Now, at home and out of office, he had no reason to act.

While he faced his customary tough challenge as the underdog in the campaign that loomed before him, two events occurred which helped transform him into a national personality. In 1831, James Kirke Paulding produced his play *The Lion of the West; or, A Trip to Washington,* featuring as its main character a certain "Nimrod Wildfire," an uneducated frontier colonel seeking public office. The play did not precisely chronicle Crockett's life, nor did the lead actor, James Hackett, precisely portray the congressman, but there were enough similarities for theatergoers to make the connection: Nimrod Wildfire became the outlandish frontier *type* that people had come to identify as David Crockett. Paulding realized that his play could only succeed through such a connection and had requested a friend, John W. Jarvis, a writer of stories about Wildfire-type characters, to share some anecdotes about the congressman's activities in Washington, and to invent some if he had to. Newspapers were quick to report that Crockett had inspired the play, prompting Paulding to write and assure the Tennessean that he did not aim to portray his life in the production. Crockett responded, telling the playwright that he had never seen the newspaper articles and that even if he had, he would not have identified himself with the Wildfire character.

Then, in January 1833, a book, *Life and Adventures of Colonel David Crockett of West Tennessee,* appeared, possibly written by Matthew St. Clair Clarke, the clerk of the House of Representatives. A member of the Clay-Adams political camp, Clarke had befriended the Tennessean early in his career and enjoyed hearing the stories of his friend's life and adventures in the wilderness. The two got along well and in 1832 traveled together for a time while Crockett visited Washington and Philadelphia. In their travels, Crockett may have shared information with Clarke, but the debate continues on whether or not Clarke actually wrote and published the volume. (Some attribute it to a Virginian, James Strange French, who may have gleaned anecdotes about Crockett from Clarke.) In any event, Crockett did not like the finished product and denied any connection with it. While it included actual episodes from his life, the book also contained some tall tales, popular at the time, and portrayed the subject as a crude, uneducated backwoodsman— the very image from which Crockett sought to detach himself. Nonetheless, the book proved popular and within months a reprint,, under the title *Sketches and Eccentricities of Colonel David Crockett of West Tennessee,* appeared in New York. Crockett could not tolerate the inaccuracies in the publication and disavowed all knowledge of the work's authorship and any complicity in writing it. To a man with a large family, constantly in debt and barely making ends meet, the realization that someone else made money by marketing his life's story also touched a nerve and he resolved to do something about it.

While the real David Crockett temporarily dropped from the public's eye, his fictional and semifictional personas via *Lion of the West* and *Sketches and Eccentricities* kept interest in him alive and endeared him to people he had never met. Those who met him were quick to fall under the spell of his carefree style and general good humor.

William L. Foster, the son of Senator Ephraim Foster, Jackson's private secretary during the Creek War, remembered Crockett as "a pleasant, courteous, and interesting man, who, though uneducated in books was a man of fine instincts and intellect, and entertained a laudable ambition to make his mark in the world. He was a man of high sense of honor, of good morals, not intemperate, nor a gambler." Ben P. Poore, later author of *Perley's Reminiscences of Sixty Years in the National Metropolis,* described Crockett as "a true frontiersman, with a small dash of shrewdness transplanted in political life." The *New York Sun* saw him as "a gentleman, his speech flashing with wit, but never vulgar or buffoonish."

As early as 1829, the *Jackson Tennessee Gazette,* while describing him as "somewhat eccentric" and suffering from a "deficit in education," stated, "His stump speeches are not famous for polish and refinement—yet they are plain, forcible and generally respectful." Ben P. Poore pointed out that "he was neither grammatical not graceful, but no rudeness of language can disguise strong sense and shrewdness." The strongly Whig *Niles Register* reported Crockett to be "an original in everything, in the tone and structure of his sentences, in the force and novelty of his metaphors, and his range of ideas." The *Little Rock Arkansas Advocate* added that his remarks were "few, plain, moderate and unaffected—without violence or acrimony," and "simply rough, natural and pleasant." The *New York Sunday Morning News* reported, "His voice was loud and well suited for stump oratory. If his vocabulary was scanty, he was master of the slang of his vernacular, and was happy in his coarse figures. He spurned the idle rules of the grammarians, and had a rhetoric of his own."

Crockett reached people through his speech-making and storytelling skills. History has misinterpreted the latter to mean he enthralled crowds with elaborate yarn spinning but his reputation as a storyteller rests upon his life experiences, enhanced by his personal brand of humor. The stories themselves were unremarkable but his presentation held people's attention. One listener in 1830 stated, "No matter what we may say of the merits of a story it is a very rare production which does not derive its interest more from the manner than the matter." Artist John Gadsby Chapman, who painted Crockett's portrait in 1834, remarked that his "command of verbal expression was very remarkable, say what he might, his meaning could never be misrepresented. He expressed opinions, and told stories, with unhesitating clearness of diction, often embellished with graphic touches of original wit and humor, sparkling, and even startling, yet never out of place or obtrusively ostentatious."

John Swisher, a Texas settler and farmer who later encountered Crockett in Texas, reported, "Few could eclipse him in conversation. He was fond of talking, and had an ease and grace about him which, added to his strong natural sense and the fund of anecdotes that he had gathered, rendered him irresistible." Swisher described his stories as "commonplace and amounted to nothing in themselves, but his inimitable way of telling them would convulse one with laughter."

The Tennessean's physical appearance could impress, surprise, or disappoint if the observer based his expectations on the literary or stage persona. A young woman, Helen Chapman, found he did not fulfill his fictional image. "He is wholly different from what I thought him," she said, describing him as "tall in stature and large in frame, but quite thin, with black hair combed straight over the forehead, parted in the middle and his shirt collar turned negligently back over his coat. He has a rather indolent appearance and looks not like a 'go ahead' man." The *Cincinnati Mirror and Western Gazette of Literature* described Crockett as "about six feet high—stoutly built—his hands and feet particularly small for a man of his appearance and character. . . . His complexion was swarthy; his cheek bones high; his nose large, and designed to favor an Indian's. His hair was long, dark and curly looking, rather uncombed than carefully attended to." A Tennessee neighbor, John L. Jacobs, remembered him as "about six feet high, weighed about two hundred pounds, had no surplus flesh, broad shouldered, stood erect, was a man of great physical strength, of fine appearance, his cheeks mantled with a rosy hue, eyes vivacious, and in form had no superior." The *Niles Register* admitted that the colonel could not be adequately described. "His leer you cannot put upon paper—his curious drawl—the odd cant of his body and his self congratulation." Those expecting a frontier "ring-tailed roarer" were sure to be disappointed. Away from home and the long hunt he did not dress as a backwoodsman. William L. Foster, who had contact with Crockett during the congressman's visits with his father, stated that he was never "attired in a garb that could be regarded as differing from that worn by gentlemen of his day—never in coon skin cap or hunting shirt." Occasionally, though, he relaxed in casual attire. The *Cincinnati*

Mirror and Western Gazette of Literature reported that while returning from a tour of the Northeast in 1834, he could be seen wearing fashionably cut pantaloons and a loose calico hunting shirt, ruffled around the collar, plus cape, cuffs, and shirt, which "set off his person as the rough and untutored woodsman, to a peculiar advantage."

Of the man himself the artist Chapman said that Crockett "rarely, if ever, exhibited either in conversation or manner, attributes of coarseness of character that prevailing popular opinion very unjustly assigned to him. I cannot recall to mind an instance of his indulgence of gasconade or profanity." A physician, S. H. Stout, remembered fondly, as a child, seeing Crockett at the Presbyterian church in Nashville. "I was in the pew immediately in front," Dr. Stout said. "My admiration of his character, engendered by what I had heard of him, and my childish curiosity got the better of the politeness I had been taught, and I turned around and looked at him steadily until with a nod and a smile, he indicated that he was more amused than offended. I have never forgotten his face and that smile on that occasion."

The *Niles Register* depicted him as "just such a one as you would desire to meet with, if any accident or misfortune had happened to you on the highway."

Crockett launched his next campaign in the spring of 1833 against the incumbent William Fitzgerald, who had defeated him two years earlier. While he tried to distance himself from any buffoonish image, the Jacksonians resorted to satire and ridicule against him in the form of a pamphlet entitled "The Book of Chronicles, West of the Tennessee and East of the

Mississippi Rivers." The author, Adam Huntsman, a west Tennessee lawyer and politician, parodied Crockett's fight for his land bill and his seduction by the Whigs in an inflated biblical prose style. He urged voters to abandon the candidate whom he portrayed as "David—a mighty man in the river country." Huntsman wrote that since "David hath beguiled us, we will desert him, and stick to Andrew, who hath brought us out of British bondage—and we will vote for William, whose surname is Fitzgerald—and the people all said, Amen!"

While Crockett dismissed the pamphlet as "foolish stuff," his opponents in the legislature also attempted to engineer his defeat by gerrymandering his electoral district so that he would be forced to run in Madison County, an area which had previously voted against him. Enough of his constituents saw through the tactic and, as he later wrote, were not disposed to be "transferred like hogs, and horses, and cattle in the market." In August 1833 he squeaked through the election by 173 votes and returned to Washington.

When the House convened the following December, Crockett immediately launched into work on the land bill, introducing a motion to appoint a select committee, which he would head, to investigate the best method of disposing of the lands in west Tennessee, and another requiring all written matter relevant to the land bill in the House to be turned over to the committee. Both proposals passed, giving him hope for passage of the bill itself.

Jackson had been reelected in 1832 with Martin Van Buren, a man whom Crockett despised, as his vice president and heir-apparent, and the Whigs immediately attacked Jackson's removal of certain deposits from the Bank of the United States, maneuvered between sessions of Congress. Jackson hated the bank, a private corporation and Whig stronghold amounting to a government-sponsored monopoly, and vowed to abolish it. When the bank's manager, Nicholas Biddle, and Henry Clay attempted to use the question of its recharter as an election issue in 1832, Jackson vetoed the recharter measure and in 1833 ordered government funds to be deposited in state banks. Crockett naturally opposed the president on this issue as he did on all others, even though his constituents looked upon the bank as a privileged tool of the wealthy in the East. He also had personal reasons for his opposition. Biddle's institution proved especially liberal with loans to its supporters, and Crockett did not hesitate while applying for an extension of a previous loan to remind the bank that he supported its recharter.

In the meantime he and other Whigs railed at Jackson as "King Andrew the First," referred to him as a tyrant, and spoke of the current administration as a "government of one man."

In addition to his ever-present land bill, Crockett had a number of other pressing matters on his mind at the time, all having to do with his growing national renown. Before the new Congress convened, he had been approached by the Whig contingent of Mississippi for permission to offer his name as a presidential candidate in 1836. The delegation explained that they needed a candidate as popular as Jackson in the West to counter the New Yorker, Van Buren, in the next election. While Crockett did not succumb to this heady offer, he did dream that his election would prove to be the perfect revenge against the Jacksonian Democrats and a way of finally resolving the land question for the poor of Tennessee.

With impossible thoughts of the White House swimming

in his head, he began writing his autobiography with some editorial assistance from Thomas Chilton, a Whig member of Congress representing Kentucky, and fellow boarder at Mrs. Ball's. Crockett sought to address the inaccuracies about his life that appeared in *Sketches and Eccentricities,* the "catchpenny errors" about "my appearance, habits, language, and everything else from that deceptive work." The impact of the book amazed him. People who read it, he said, "have almost in every instance expressed the most profound astonishment at finding me in human shape, and with countenance, appearance, and common feelings of a human being." He began writing his own book in December 1833, immediately after Congress convened, and on January 10, 1834, wrote to his son John Wesley that he had already completed 110 pages of a projected two hundred. He enthusiastically described letters from interested publishers in New York and Philadelphia, and wrote of a possible promotional tour through the Northeast during the congressional recess. Those who urged him to take the tour assured him that his presence before the public would induce thousands to buy the book. He needed the sales to relieve perpetual indebtedness, informing his son, "I intend never to go home until I am able to pay all my debts and I think I have a good prospect at present and I will do the best I can." He intended to take advantage of his growing status as an American celebrity. "Go where I will, everybody seems anxious to get a peep at me," he wrote. "There must therefore be something in me, or about me, that attracts attention, which is even mysterious to myself."

In February 1834, he contracted with the Philadelphia publishing firm of Carey and Hart and reacted with all the enthusiasm of a fledgling author. He showered the publishers with suggestions on marketing, book length, print and margin size, and requests for author's copies. He knew that the publishers would make editorial adjustments to the manuscript but he requested they not make too many corrections to his language since he did not want to detract from his frontier prose style.

The book, *A Narrative of the Life of David Crockett of the State of Tennessee,* became an instant success when published in March, its first printing selling out in three weeks. The author devoted most of the work to his impoverished childhood, his experiences in the Creek War, his hunting adventures, and his crafty electioneering victories. Very little space described his actual legislative duties or his land bill problems. His few political references were limited to tongue-in-cheek swipes at Jackson and the removal of government funds from the Bank of the United States, Crockett's independence as a politician, and how all the power of the Democratic party had lined up against him as a result. He ended the book by assuring his readers that he would never wear a collar with the inscription "My Dog— Andrew Jackson," but that he would be found standing up "as the people's faithful representative, and the public's, most obedient, very humble servant."

Except for the publisher's decision to edit out many references to brutality against the Indians during the Creek War, and those Crockett identified as responsible for such treatment, he was pleased with the book. The receipts from its sale, while not solving all of his financial burdens, brought in some much needed money. More important, it gained him a growing and appreciative audience.

As his notoriety spread, the line between fact and fiction, and life and legend, continued to blur in the public's perception of him. In December 1833, he had the opportunity of catching a benefit performance by James Hackett at the Washington Theater. At the congressman's request Hackett performed scenes from Paulding's *Lion of the West*, adding an unforgettable moment for theatergoers when the actor took the stage in his Colonel Nimrod Wildfire costume and bowed to Crockett, who rose from his box seat and returned the bow to the delight and thunderous applause of the audience.

As he became more entranced by his public image, he began spending as much time cultivating it as he did on his legislative duties. He simply enjoyed the attention and, if not fully understanding it, saw no reason not to use it to his advantage. To his constituents of west Tennessee he remained "the gentleman from the cane"—one of their own who had risen to represent them in the nation's capital; to the people of the east he represented the quintessential backwoods character. However he may have perceived himself, he did not willingly disappoint those who had a certain expectation of him. On one occasion he sat with some friends in his room at Mrs. Ball's boardinghouse when the proprietor announced the arrival of a man who guided tourists around Washington. The man had two visitors with him who wished to "pay their respects to Colonel Crockett." "Show 'em up, show 'em up," Crockett said while slouching in his seat, throwing his leg over the arm of the chair, and donning a hat. He shook hands with the visitors without rising, welcomed them with some homey, west Tennessee greetings, and as the visitors made themselves comfortable, eased into a few of his best stories. When he finished he bid his visitors farewell with cordial handshakes and wishes for a safe and pleasant journey home. As soon as the admirers had left the room Crockett replaced his hat on the table and announced, "Well!—they came to see a 'bar,' and they've seen one—hope they like the performance—it did not cost them anything any how—Let's take a horn."

Good Nonsense

Crockett's tour of the Northeast in the spring of 1834, while proving his standing as a celebrity and public figure, also proved to be the undoing of his political career. He had written to his son about the possibility of such a tour once the current legislative session ended, but could not restrain himself from starting early—on April 25, during the height of activity in the House. The Whigs planned and choreographed the whirlwind, nineteen-day trip with stops in Baltimore, Philadelphia, New York City, Boston and Lowell, Massachusetts; Newport and Providence, Rhode Island; and Jersey City and Camden, New Jersey.

The Whigs needed a Western alternative to the president and his successor, Van Buren, to present to the people in the East, and they also needed a somewhat politically expendable person who could draw crowds and deliver a strongly worded anti-administration diatribe with impunity. Crockett simply wanted to meet people, promote his book, and generally have a good time. He basked in the attention at first, making anti-Jackson speeches, shaking hands, visiting manufacturing centers, attending patriotic ceremonies, and accepting gifts all along the way. Organizations of young Whigs wined and dined him, and delighted in his attacks against the president in which he described Jackson as a tyrant with a sword in one hand and the country's purse in the other, and likened him to King George III.

He began his tour with a night's stay at Barnum's Hotel in Baltimore, then continued on to Philadelphia by steamboat, where an enthusiastic mob greeted him. Here his sponsors established a pattern for the remainder of his trip, taking him to public and private institutions, giving him the opportunity to entertain crowds with his anti-Jackson speech, and allowing him to enjoy hospitality wherever he stopped. He stayed at the United States Hotel on Chestnut Street, ironically, or perhaps intentionally, directly across from the Bank of the United States, from which Jackson had so recently removed the funds. On the following morning he toured the city, making stops at an asylum, the Mint, and the waterworks. Later in the day his escorts invited him to the newly constructed stock exchange for a speech. He agreed but immediately regretted his decision when he came in sight of the place and found the streets lined with more than five thousand people. "I have faced the enemy," he later wrote, and while reassuring himself that these were his friends, said, "I'll keep cool and let them have it." A young boy in the crowd bolstered his spirits by shouting, "Go ahead, Davy Crockett." His Jackson attack went over well, earning him three cheers three times upon its completion, after which he spent an hour shaking hands with his appreciative listeners.

In the evening he attended a theater where the audience paid more attention to him than to the show, dutifully laughing whenever he did. He found at stops all along his trip people thronging "to see the wild man," and came to the conclusion that he would "rather be in the wilderness with my gun and dogs, than to be attracting all that fuss." He found the performance not totally to his liking since "theater" at the time could not be mistaken for genteel culture. "I have heard some things in them that was a leetle too tough for good women and modest men; and that's a great pity," he wrote. "There are thousands of scenes of real life that might be exhibited, both for amusement and edification, without offending."

He continued his tour of the city over the next two days, during which he accepted gifts from his admirers—a watch chain engraved "Go Ahead," and the promise of a fine new rifle, made to his specifications, from the Young Whigs of Philadelphia. On April 30, he boarded the steamboat *New Philadelphia* for passage up the Delaware River, then by train to Amboy, New Jersey, and finally by boat again to New York City, which he described as "a bulger of a place." He stood in awe of the ships in New York Harbor as he had during his boyhood journey to Baltimore many years before. The forest of masts in the harbor still impressed him, looking "for all the world like a big clearing in the West, with the dead trees all standing."

After registering at the American Hotel he stopped to view a new and elegant fire apparatus and have some refreshments with the firefighters in charge of it. Later, he watched the performance of the actress Fanny Kemble at the Park Theater, finding the show and ambience more pleasing than his Philadelphia experience. He may have been influenced by Miss Kemble's beauty, describing her as a "handsome piece of changeable silk; first one color, than another, but always the clean thing."

That evening, while he and some friends sat around the hotel chatting, somebody outside yelled "Fire!" Crockett jumped up and ran for his hat, prepared to help fight the blaze. "Sit down, Colonel," one of his amused companions said. "We have fire companies here, and we leave it to them." The bewildered die-hard volunteer reflected later, "At home I would have jumped on the first horse at hand, and rode full flight bare-backed, to help put out a fire." Still, his curiosity got the best of him and he and one of the men went out to the scene. While in Philadelphia he had been fascinated by the waterworks and its ability to pump great volumes of water for firefighting purposes and remembered, "As for a fire, it has no chance at all: they just screw on a long hollow leather with a brass nose on it, dash up stairs, and seem to draw on Noah's flood." Now, he had the opportunity to see the equipment in action: "The engines were only assembling when we got there; but when they began to spirt, they put out a four-story house that was all in a blaze in less than no time."

The next morning he visited the newspaper offices of the *Morning Courier and New York Enquirer* and *The Star,* preferring the *Courier and Enquirer*'s editor, James Watson Webb, to Mordecai M. Noah of *The Star,* saying that Webb "comes out plump with what he has to say." He strolled along Pearl Street, saw the stock exchange, and visited Peale's Museum, failing to comprehend what "pleasure or curiosity folks could take in sticking up whole rows of little bugs, and such like varmints." He met New York City mayor Gideon Lee at City Hall and dined with Seba Smith, author of a series of political letters for newspapers written under the name Major Jack Downing, an imaginary Crockett-like character.

The following day brought more visits to newspaper offices, a trip uptown, and a tour of the Five Points area of the East Side with James Webb. This notorious section of the Sixth Ward, a Van Buren Democratic stronghold, shocked the Tennessean, whose denizens he found "too mean to swab hell's kitchen," admitting that he "would rather risque myself in an Indian fight than venture among these creatures after night." He later enjoyed a more pleasant time taking part in a flag-raising at the Battery on the southern tip of Manhattan, returning to his hotel exhausted. There he found a handbill from the Bowery theater announcing, to his annoyance, since he had not been asked, that he would be there. As showtime drew near the managers of the theater sent for him, but he refused to budge, and when the nervous head of the theater appeared in person to beg Crockett to attend, the tired and cranky celebrity informed the manager that he "did not come for the citizens of New York to look at, I come to look at them." He only relented when his friends explained what a great disappointment it would be, and how dangerous it could become for the managers if he did not appear. He attended for a short time, took his bows, and enjoyed a welcome reception from the crowd, finally returning to his hotel with a greater understanding of the real purpose of his tour.

On the morning of May 3, Crockett crossed the Hudson River to Jersey City to watch a shooting match and joined in. At one hundred yards and with an unfamiliar rifle, he put a ball within two inches of the target's center. After explaining that he normally shot from forty yards, he moved closer to the target and fired with more success. When his host placed a coin in the center of the bull's-eye, ignoring the warning to save his money, Crockett fired again, making "slight-of-hand work with his quarter."

Back in New York, he caught the 3:30 P.M. steamboat for Boston, passing through the tricky currents of Hell's Gate at the northwest end of Long Island, and into Long Island Sound. After short stops in Newport and Providence, Rhode Island, he caught a stage for Boston, covering the forty miles in only four hours, took accommodations at the Tremont House, and enjoyed celebrity treatment for the duration of his stay. His tour continued in Boston, where he visited sites such as the U.S.S. *Constitution,* "Old Ironsides," in dry dock, and met the artist Chester Harding, with whom he agreed to sit for a portrait. During a side trip to Roxborough, he visited a garment factory that made clothing treated with India rubber, receiving a water-resistant hunting coat as a gift. He became an advocate of Yankee ingenuity and industry, a stance pleasing to his Whig hosts, who hoped he would bring this message back to his constituents in the West.

The battle by colonial forces against professional British soldiers at Bunker Hill especially inspired him. On what he considered hallowed ground he contemplated how he could help protect the liberty and freedom they had fought and sacrificed for, resolving "as I had done elsewhere, to go for my country always and everywhere."

Public interest in him never abated. On the evening of his first full day in Boston he turned down a half dozen invitations in order to fulfill his obligation to dine with a group of one hundred young Whigs who treated him to sumptuous fare. He drank champagne for the first time, likening it to "supping fog out of speaking trumpets," and in keeping with the established pattern of the trip, he thanked his hosts for their hospitality with his anti-Jackson speech. In the morning he took a leisurely stroll through the city, gawking at the sites like any tourist. He found a representation of a large codfish hanging in the House of Assembly especially amusing; a statue of George Washington in the State House displeased him since the artist had chosen to portray the president in a Roman toga. "He belonged to *this* country—heart, soul, and body: and I don't want any other to have any part of him—not even his clothes," he observed.

In the afternoon, he visited an institution for the blind at the invitation of the school's master, who sent a blind boy to escort him there. Crockett came away amazed at the boy's ability to lead him through the city, as well as the other students' skills in reading and arithmetic, accomplished by feeling upraised letters and numbers with their fingers. He refused an invitation to visit Cambridge, where he knew that honorary degrees were sometimes bestowed, fearing that someone would stick an "LL.D." on the end of his name, which he felt could be interpreted by some to mean "Lazy, Lounging Dunce." Dinner and the theater rounded out his evening again, but the novelty of both had begun to wear off. He pointed out that an older actress portraying the part of a young lady looked to be either "a married woman," or "who had ought to be," and an actor who delivered a song proved to have a voice "not half up to a Mississippi boat-horn." The fact that the theater was a temperance institution and patrons could not get a drink there did not help his grumpy disposition. As soon as he and his friends realized this, they adjourned to the Tremont House, where the proprietor, Crockett said, "keeps stuff that runs friends together, and makes them forget which is which," and there cleansed the taste of the theater from their palates.

A heavy rain prevented him from visiting the manufacturing center at Lowell, Massachusetts, on the following day, keeping him confined to his hotel, where he mingled with other guests. On May 8, the weather cleared enough for him to make his scheduled trip. Five thousand women and young girls, a "mile of gals," he said, worked in Lowell, a manufacturing town, and he met and mingled with them. Impressed by the females working efficiently and contentedly at a variety of jobs, including the operation of machinery, he compared them with the women of other countries, where the "female character is degraded to abject slavery."

After an overnight stay he returned to Boston, spending an evening at the home of the lieutenant governor, Samuel T. Armstrong, then going off again to the theater. The weary congressman behaved so quietly and gentlemanly at the show that he felt he had disappointed the audience, who expected to see a "half horse, half alligator sort of fellow."

He left Boston won over by its friendship and generosity—especially after discovering that the management of the Tremont refused pay for his stay there, as had the proprietor of his lodging in Lowell. He returned to New York, "that city of eternal din and confusion," and then back to Philadelphia and a short return trip to Camden, New Jersey, where another crowd awaited him. He spent a pleasant afternoon there, spoiled only by the fact that he and some of his companions fell victim to a pickpocket while they mingled. He remained philosophical about the incident, speculating that it must have been done by a Jackson man. On the morning of May 11, he returned to Baltimore by steamboat, then by stage to Washington, where he reluctantly resumed his congressional duties.

The Whigs had used the trip to test his popularity in the East, and used him to drive home their anti-Jackson message. Whether he realized to what extent they manipulated him is not known. Arriving worn out in Washington during the second week of May, his darkening mood worsened when he received a letter from John Wesley, who had recently "gotten religion," chastising his father about his excesses. He complained that his son thought himself "off to Paradise on a streak of lightening," and who, he said, "pitches into me pretty considerable."

He returned to the House fueled by the attention of the people he met and the enthusiastic support of the Whigs who had joined him on every leg of his journey, but was frustrated by his lack of success in Congress. He attacked Jackson and his supporters with renewed energy, his tirades becoming increasingly tiresome to his colleagues. The tedium of the House and lack of movement on anything meaningful to him also began to take their toll. During a debate that had brought a large crowd to the capitol, he escaped the building and met John Gadsby Chapman on the Pennsylvania Avenue side. Chapman remarked that the congressman looked as if he had just delivered a long speech. "Long Speech to thunder, there's plenty of 'em up there for that sort of nonsense, without making a fool of myself at public expense," Crockett said. "I can stand *good nonsense*—rather like it— but such nonsense as they are digging at up yonder, it's no use trying to—I'm going home."

He could be frank with Chapman, the two becoming well acquainted while the artist labored over Crockett's portrait. A number of likenesses of the Tennessean already had been painted, the earliest in 1827, when he first entered the national scene, and several others more recently. His sudden interest in preserving an accurate portrait of himself may have had to do with an awareness of his growing celebrity. He sat for no less than six portraits by five different artists between 1833 and 1834.

Chapman, of Alexandria, Virginia, began painting the last images of the congressman in Washington in May 1834. His bust portrait is romanticized, portraying a relaxed and somewhat dashing subject in an open-collared shirt. It still did not satisfy Crockett, who recognized how well his frontier image played with his throngs of admirers in the East. Upon seeing the painting he told Chapman, "Dare say its like enough, because it's like all the other painters make of me, a sort of cross between a clean shirted Member of Congress and a Methodist Preacher." He added, "If you could catch me on a bear-hunt in a 'harrican,' with hunting tools and gear, and team of dogs, you might make a picture better worth looking at."

Chapman admitted a lack of knowledge of such scenes, and expressed a reluctance to impose on his subject for any further sittings. The idea took shape, however, and when the artist produced a rough preliminary sketch, Crockett jumped into the project enthusiastically, scouring Washington for authentic equipment and props. He acquired an old linsey-woolsey hunting shirt, leggings, moccasins, butcher knife, and hatchet. He rejected rifles if they appeared too new or ornate. Finally he found and borrowed a well-worn piece belonging to an old hunter on the Potomac River. He populated the scene with three mongrels from the streets of Washington to represent his own hunting dogs, and only consented to allow Chapman's own trained and well-bred dog in the painting on the condition that it be "stuck into one corner," and with its "playful tail" out of sight.

Even with the proper accoutrements, the static composition of the painting, posed with Crockett standing stiffly and wearing a wide-brimmed hat, did not appeal to the subject. Chapman sensed his uneasiness but did not know the cause until Crockett entered the studio one morning, waved his hat in the air, and let out a yell that "raised the whole neighborhood."

His dramatic entrance inspired Chapman to alter the painting, giving his subject a more dynamic pose. The full-length portrait shows Crockett in hunting garb, with hatchet and butcher knife arranged on his belt in easy reach, his shot pouch and powder horn hanging from his left shoulder and resting on his right hip, with the four dogs grouped around him. The artist, who had studied in Rome, posed Crockett in a style reminiscent of some classical sculptures, with his right hand raised, holding his hat, and his rifle cradled in his left arm, his face and body illuminated as if by the setting sun. The portrait gives the impression that Crockett is waving farewell to the East for the last time, and is about to turn his face westward, an impression that would prove prophetic.

Chapman's work pleased Crockett more than any of the previous attempts, and the congressman remained very protective of it. When the artist exhibited the painting in New York City the following year, a prominent literary friend of his remarked that Crockett did not appear to know how to arrange his hatchet on his belt, and that the picture should be altered. The outraged Tennessean fired back a reply: "Do'nt you go to altering my picture for any body's nonsense. If any man in New York says I do'nt know how, or where, to stick my hatchet, send him to me and I'le show him."

When Crockett returned to Congress in May, he found the

House preparing for adjournment but slipped in during a vote and surprised the other representatives when he answered to his name.

He was anxious to leave again and wrote of looking toward adjournment "as ever did a poor convict in the penitentiary to see his last day come." With less than a month remaining in the session, he knew that he would not be able to accomplish anything in the interests of his constituents and so spent most of his time on the floor attacking Jackson and Van Buren. He spitefully opposed anything their supporters endorsed, no matter how inconsequential, including Polk's proposal to extend the House's adjournment date by two weeks. He opposed this measure even though it would have given him more time to work on his bill, but Congress voted for it anyway, extending the session until June 30.

Crockett suffered through most of the extension, but could not bring himself to stay to the end. On June 29 he left Washington to put the final touches on his Eastern tour, arriving in Philadelphia on the thirtieth, and on the following day accepting the fine rifle promised him by the Young Whigs, together with a hunting knife and tomahawk. At the presentation ceremony he assured his admirers that no rifle he ever handled could compare with the new one in beauty, and should it become necessary, promised to use it in defense of the liberty of the country. In the morning he test-fired the weapon at Camden, shooting reasonably well since he had been out of practice for a while, but having no doubt about the quality of the firearm. "The fault would be mine if the varmints did not suffer," once man and rifle became better acquainted, he said.

On July 4, he took part in a daylong Independence Day

celebration in the company of a number of prominent Whig legislators, including Daniel Webster. He mingled with the crowds, enjoyed cool drinks, a fine dinner, and listened to a reading of the Declaration of Independence. He fulfilled his role in the ceremonies by delivering his anti-Jackson litany several times during the day. Two days later he boarded a train for Pittsburgh, collecting more gifts before departing—a dozen cannisters of gunpowder from manufacturer E. I. Dupont for use with his new rifle, and a pitcher, courtesy of a china importer, for Mrs. Crockett. On the steamboat *Hunter,* after stops at Wheeling, and Guyandotte, Virginia, he arrived in Cincinnati on July 12 and delivered his obligatory speech before continuing on to Louisville. The following morning he took a short side trip to speak at Jeffersonville Springs, Indiana, then returned to Louisville that evening, where he addressed what was described to him as the "largest concourse of people that ever has been assembled in Louisville since it has been settled." After his stay, he boarded the steamboat *Scotland,* gratefully stepping foot on Tennessee soil at Mill's Point on July 22. His son William met him there and they drove a wagon the last thirty-five miles to his home in Gibson County.

Hell and Texas

rockett spent the rest of the summer uneventfully, struggling with his financial problems. In the early fall, John Crockett, who had followed his son to west Tennessee, died, and David spent much of his time at home acting as the administrator of his father's estate.

He had not been home long before the Democratic press leveled accusations against him. Crockett had attacked Jackson and Van Buren freely during his tour and his speeches were reproduced in a number of newspapers; now, the other side countered, questioning his absence from Congress in April and May, asking him to justify his congressional salary while absent, and mocking him as a fool and buffoon of the Whigs. He had no answers for these charges and lamely fell back on the defense he had used before the tour—that he had been suffering from chest pains and had to travel for his health. It is unlikely that anyone believed this excuse but this did not concern him; his reelection bid would come the following summer and by then, he was certain, the charges against him would be forgotten, particularly if he could guide his land bill through the legislative process. In the meantime he had more pressing concerns, chief among them his rising indebtedness. At some point before Congress convened in December 1834, he came to an agreement with William Clark, a Whig representative from Pennsylvania and another boarder at Mrs. Ball's, to put the details of his Northeastern tour into book form. Once again he entered into a contract with Carey and Hart, which had published his autobiography, and almost immediately began haranguing the company for advances as well as for royalty payments on his previous work.

The Tennessean agreed that Clark would put the manuscript into publishable form while Crockett's role involved conveying his memories and impressions of the trip to Clark, and collecting newspaper accounts from the stops along the way as source material. He worked on his portion of the book through December and most of January and, while not wholly neglecting his congressional duties, he certainly diverted much of his attention from them. He completed his task before the end of January 1835, and began planning and corresponding with Carey and Hart about another book, a satiric biography of Martin Van Buren.

As in the past, he began the congressional session with a strong effort on behalf of his west Tennessee constituents, and met with his usual lack of success. In frustration he became more cantankerous than ever on the floor of the House, opposing any measures brought up by the Jackson camp. Even his Whig friends tired of his obstructionist ways, abandoning any idea of his presidential potential. After two and a half terms he was essentially a one-bill congressman who could not get that bill passed. He had no legislative successes to build a campaign around, and had simply proved too difficult to handle. Since he had not surrendered to party politics with his fellow Tennesseans under Jackson and the Democrats, the Whigs had little reason to believe that he would be faithful to their party.

During his time in Congress, due to his vocal opposition to Jackson, it is unlikely that Crockett had many personal encounters with the president, a circumstance that changed on January 30, 1835, at a congressional funeral held in the capital when both men were present and within a few feet of each other. As Jackson left the House chambers, an unemployed house painter named Richard Lawrence, who believed himself heir to the British throne and was convinced that the president had murdered his father, leveled two cap-and-ball pistols at Jackson's chest and pulled the triggers. Miraculously, both guns misfired and the sixty-seven-year-old president, wielding his cane as a weapon, started toward the madman. Some of the younger men present, including Crockett, moved faster and subdued the would-be assassin. "I wanted to see the damnedest villain in the world—and now I have seen him," Crockett said after the struggle.

If he ever seriously thought of a run for the presidency, such an idea, impossible in any event, evaporated when Martin Van Buren received Jackson's fullest endorsement to succeed to the presidency. He appeared unbeatable. That Jackson could handpick his successor, in seeming defiance of the free electoral process, further enraged Crockett, and with the Whigs continuing to be cool toward him, he entered into a back-room arrangement. This involved endorsing, as did most of the Tennessee delegation, Senator Hugh Lawson White, a former Jackson friend and supporter, as the Democratic nominee against Van

Buren. Only three of Jackson's staunchest supporters, including future president James K. Polk, were absent from this plot, an arrangement the president viewed as the greatest of betrayals, not only to himself but to the Democratic party. He began demanding that "Crockett and Co." be "hurled, as they ought, from the confidence of the people."

Since his election to Congress in 1827, Crockett's main efforts had been toward making the land in west Tennessee available and affordable to the people who settled and tamed it. He spent his last days in Congress stubbornly fighting for this single issue, delivering his last speech on behalf of his land bill on February 20, 1835. His last recorded vote on the floor of the House came on March 3, not surprisingly cast in opposition to a measure that Andrew Jackson favored, a vote that proved unsuccessful. Congress adjourned that day and he returned to Tennessee with the responsibility of another campaign weighing on him. His political future and a last chance at providing some substantial benefit for the people he represented depended on this election.

In March 1835, Carey and Hart published *An Account of Col. Crockett's Tour to the North and Down East in the Year of Our Lord One Thousand Eight Hundred and Thirty Four,* "Written by Himself." Although some of the book contained Crockett's own records and observations of his trip, most of it was political, boosting his reelection campaign as well as the Whig cause in general. William Clark included no less than ten repetitions of Crockett's anti-Jackson speech in various forms as delivered on the tour. In June, *The Life of Martin Van Buren, Heir-apparent to the Government and the Appointed Successor of General Jackson* followed, with Crockett listed as the author, the book actually written by another Whig friend, Senator Augustin Smith Clayton of Georgia. The publishers, Carey and Hart, concerned about the possibility of libel, kept their names off the volume but retained Crockett's since he already had gone so far out on a limb against the administration.

One other publication, significant to Crockett's life and legend, appeared at this time, the first of a series of *Davy Crockett Almanacs,* which portrayed him as a frontier wildman involved in outlandish adventures. Published in the East, the series ran for twenty years, forty-five volumes of increasingly violent tall tales, illustrated by crude woodcuts. Crockett had nothing to do with these works and made nothing from their publication. They served only to help bury the man under a growing mythology.

The gentleman from the cane once again took to the campaign trail, on the defensive. Adam Huntsman, also known as "Black Hawk," the Tennessee lawyer who had ridiculed Crockett in *The Book of Chronicles* some years earlier, challenged him for the seat. Although a committed Jackson man, Huntsman was not Crockett's enemy; the lawyer, in fact, had represented the congressman only a few months earlier in a court case involving the executorship of the estate of Robert Patton, Crockett's father-in-law. Now, however, Crockett defended himself before the voters against a variety of charges: inflating his mileage expenses for travel to and from Washington; abusing the congressional franking privilege by sending anti-Jackson material to his constituents but ignoring their requests for pro-Jackson literature; absenteeism; and, his biggest stumbling block, failure to get his land bill passed. He fought back but could not escape the picture that the opposition painted of him—that of a traitor to Andrew Jackson and, ultimately, to Tennessee.

On occasion he was able to fend off the charges long enough to show some of his old flair during the campaign. As in the past, he and his opponent traveled together on their stump tour, usually lodging together. On one such tour they stayed at the cabin of a farmer who happened to have a grown daughter, sharing a room down a wooden walkway from that of the girl. Once everyone was soundly asleep, Crockett decided to playfully exploit two of Huntsman's vulnerable points: the fact that the lawyer had a peg leg, having lost the limb in the War of 1812, and his reputed weakness for the ladies. Crockett sneaked out of their room, armed with a wooden chair, and walked to the girl's door, rattling it as if trying to enter and making sure she woke up. She did, raising a noisy protestation, while Crockett hobbled down the walkway, banging his chair against the floor with every other step, sounding for all to hear like a wooden-legged man beating a retreat. In the ensuing furor Crockett intervened on Huntsman's behalf, without implicating himself, saving his opponent and winning the farmer's vote.

As satisfying as the prank may have been it proved woefully insufficient at the polls. Crockett wrote that he could "handle the Administration without gloves," and facetiously predicted that he would be writing yet another book—"The Second Fall of Adam,"—referring to Adam Huntsman, but the voters let him know that he had fallen from their confidence, giving his opponent 252 more votes in the August election. The outcome turned on the fact that their congressman had nothing to show for his three terms and that it had become obvious to many voters that their interests would be better served if someone less antagonistic to the administration represented them.

Crockett thus watched his political career end. Huntsman

went off to Washington, and the country, Congress, and politics moved ahead while the former representative languished in west Tennessee. His defeat actually may have been a relief since it freed him from the demands of electioneering, the formalities of Washington, and the endless tedium of speeches and debates on the House floor.

For a while he had been casting a restless eye west and making statements that if Van Buren became president, he would leave for Texas, then a part of a northern province of Mexico, which in 1821 had opened a portion of its rich lands to American settlement. Under the new regime of military strongman General Antonio López de Santa Anna, conditions in Texas had become increasingly restrictive, with tensions rising between the Mexican government and the American settlers, but Crockett considered any government better than one led by Martin Van Buren, undoubtedly the next president.

Texas, in fact, had been on his mind as early as 1830 when he spoke in Congress urging that the Maysville Road be extended as far as Memphis, "the direct route from this city to the province of Texas." He reflected the thoughts of many in the United States when he hoped that Texas "will one day belong to the United States and that at no great distance of time."

Matilda Crockett, his youngest child, remembered her father returning home after his congressional defeat and telling his wife, "Well, Bet, I am beat and I'm off for Texas." Matilda said he wanted to move his whole family immediately but Elizabeth convinced him to proceed, look the country over, and decide if he wanted to make a home there for the family.

Before embarking he had arranged a barbecue and barn dance for family and friends, at which, Matilda recalled, "The young folks danced all day and night and everybody enjoyed themselves."

He began the journey to Texas in the company of two neighbors, Lindsy K. Tinkle and Abner Burgin, and his nephew William Patton, leaving his nineteen-year-old son Robert in charge of the family. Matilda said of her father on the morning he left, "He was dressed in his hunting suit, wearing a coon skin cap." In her last fond memory of him she stated, "He was a large, fine, portly looking man and loved to hunt and shoot at matches."

Before leaving Tennessee he wrote a letter to Elizabeth's brother, George Patton, telling him that his party intended departing the next morning, November 1, 1835, and that "we will go through Arkinsaw and I want to explore Texas well before I return."

Less than a month before this letter was written, the first shots had been fired in what would become the Texas revolution. This occurred when a small party of Mexican soldiers dispatched from San Antonio de Béxar attempted to relieve the American settlers in the town of Gonzales, seventy-five miles to the east, of a cannon loaned to them for protection against Indians. The settlers resisted, hoisted a homemade flag with "Come and Take It" painted on it, and after a small skirmish sent the Mexican troops reeling back to San Antonio. Then, only four days before the Tennessean's departure, a ragtag Texan force battled and defeated a superior number of Mexican troops at the mission Nuestra Señora de la Purísima Concepción de Acuña, just outside San Antonio.

Early in the morning of November 10, Crockett and his company arrived in Memphis, where he casually strolled the streets in relative anonymity. As he called on such old friends as Marcus B. Winchester, the news of his arrival spread. The last night he would spend in Tennessee began calmly with a dozen or so friends gathered about him for drinks, but developed into what James B. Davis, a young man on the periphery of the group, described as a "Big bender."

The well-wishers assembled in the Union Hotel but adjourned to Hart's Saloon, judged better to handle a crowd and with the liquor more accessible. The crowd was convivial until one of the revelers, the generous but short-tempered Gus Young, one of Winchester's political cronies, informed the proprietor that he would pay for the drinks—tomorrow. Crockett had to step in to separate Young and Hart when the barkeep informed all that he did not extend credit. A few of the men, including the honored guest, offered to pay, but Young refused, borrowing the money to settle the bill, then leading the assemblage to another establishment where they would be better appreciated. The crowd had grown and once outside, some of them hoisted Crockett on their shoulders and marched him a few doors down to the general store of Neil McCool, who also served liquor, and where they boosted the ex-congressman onto the counter. As liquor and talk of good times flowed freely, Crockett told his admirers that since his constituents chose not to reelect him, they could "go to hell and I'll go to Texas," a phrase he repeated in a variety of forms along the way.

His companions loved it but McCool, a "fastidious bachelor," as described by Davis, was less than pleased to see two big muddy boots stomping on the new oilcloth covering the counter. He fumed until he could take it no longer and expressed his displeasure to Gus Young, who seemed to be leading the group. The volatile Young responded by grabbing a handful of the man's hair, only to discover McCool's wig in his hand. As the crowd convulsed in laughter, the bald proprietor began hurling tumblers then vaulted the counter after Young. It took a half dozen men to restrain him but his rage was such that he threw everyone out without getting paid for the liquor they had consumed. They left peacefully but only after Young tossed McCool's wig onto a high shelf.

Once in the street the revelers debated whether to continue the party or to go home, Crockett favoring the latter. The original contingent managed to disperse a hundred or so of the more rowdy element, then broke up into smaller groups to roam the streets, eventually reassembling in front of the closed establishment of another store owner, Joseph Cooper. One of the party banged on the door crying, "Freight! Freight!" as if a delivery had arrived, rousing the sleep-addled Cooper from his bed. He opened his door long enough for twenty-five of the partygoers, including Crockett, to boil in and continue the frolic. Cooper carried the largest and best supply of liquor in Memphis but did not sell by the glass—only by the cask or keg—so the crowd bought in quantity. Crockett and a few others were called upon for speeches, keeping everyone entertained to a late hour. James Davis later recalled, "It is needless to say we all got tight—I might say, yes, very tight. Men who never were tight before, and never have been tight since, were certainly VERY TIGHT then."

However tight Crockett may have been, he loosened up enough by morning to take his leave of Memphis and his beloved state of Tennessee for the last time. He left his hotel escorted by the nucleus of his farewell party, including Marcus

B. Winchester, with Davis following them down to the ferry landing. "He wore that same veritable coon-skin cap and hunting shirt, bearing upon his shoulder his ever faithful rifle," Davis wrote. "No other equipment, save his shot-pouch and powder-horn, do I remember seeing."

Crockett and his companions boarded a ferry, crossed the river into Arkansas, and made good time through the territory. By the evening of November 12 they had arrived in Little Rock and took rooms at the Charles Jeffries City Hotel. Once again city officials organized a dinner in his honor, and when they came to the hotel to make their formal invitation, they found the famous congressman in the back of he building calmly skinning a deer he had bagged en route. He accepted their offer, attended the dinner, and entertained his hosts with a combination of his anti-Jackson and "hell and Texas" speeches. In the morning he and his party set out again, heading southwest, crossing the Red River at the settlement of Lost Prairie, Arkansas, and setting foot on Texas soil for the first time.

For the next month the travelers roamed and explored the northeast Texas countryside, visiting Big Prairie, Clarksville, and Nacogdoches, at each town Crockett enjoying celebrity treatment and delivering his now well-rehearsed speech. As usual, the Tennessean was broke so, before the party crossed over into Texas, he had traded his pocket watch with the "Go Ahead" inscription for settler Isaac Jones's watch and a balance of thirty dollars.

As they wandered, he fell under the spell of Texas and its abundant game. He and his party became so enthralled during a hunting expedition in December that they went missing for several days, causing speculation that they had been killed by Indians, which in fact was later reported in Eastern newspapers.

While Crockett and his friends enjoyed the hospitality and hunting in east Texas, monumental events were taking place to the southwest, where Texan forces had besieged a Mexican garrison under General Martín Perfecto de Cos in the town of San Antonio de Béxar. On December 5, the disorganized Texans pulled themselves together long enough to attack the town and drive the Mexican force out and into an old Spanish mission, known as the Alamo, on the opposite side of the San Antonio River. There, on December 9, Cos and his soldiers were forced to surrender, then were released under the condition that they would never again take up arms against the Mexican constitution of 1824. (Originally the Texas rebels fought for their rights under this liberal constitution, seeking statehood within the Mexican confederation but separate from that of the giant state of Coahuila y Téjas, to which they belonged. Another faction sought complete independence from Mexico, this group growing stronger as immigrants from the United States poured over the border in search of land.)

On January 8, the citizens of San Augustine, just west of the Sabine River in northeast Texas, fired a cannon to welcome Crockett and his men, offering them the celebrity treatment of dinner and speeches. The Tennessean had become a dedicated Texas convert by this time, admiring everything he saw, and winning the adulation of the people who spoke of him as representing them in a constitutional convention should they achieve their independence. While in San Augustine he wrote to his daughter Margaret and her husband, Wiley Flowers, boasting of his good health and high spirits and praising Texas as the "Garden spot of the world." He wrote of the 4,438 acres he could obtain on the Choctaw or Bois d'Arc bayous of the Red River, calling it "the richest country in the world, good land, plenty of timber, and the best springs and good mill streams, good range, clear water & every appearance of health—game a plenty."

He returned to Nacogdoches convinced that his future lay in the vast land, seeing that service in the fledgling Texan army was the quickest path to securing a land claim and a position as a framer of the future constitution. On January 12, 1836, he took an oath to serve in the Volunteer Auxiliary Corps of Texas for a six-month enlistment. Ever the legislator as well as volunteer, he refused to swear to service until the officiating judge changed the wording of the oath requiring him to support any "future government that may be thereafter declared" to any "future *republican* government."

After signing up he completed the letter to his daughter begun in San Augustine, informing his family of his decision and telling them that he would "set out for the Rio Grande in a few days with the volunteers of the U.S. . . . I am rejoiced at my fate. I had rather be in my present situation than to be elected to a seat in Congress for life."

With His Friends

Many years after his death, Crockett's daughter Matilda remembered, "We did not know that he intended going into the army until he wrote mother a letter after he got to Texas." That letter has not survived, but aware of the anxiety his enlistment would cause his family, he tried to reassure them of his safety. In his final words to daughter Margaret he wrote, "I hope you will do the best you can and I will do the same. Do not be uneasy about me, I am with my friends."

Those friends and a number of others took the oath of allegiance to Texas on the day Crockett did, but his traveling companions, Burgin and Tinkle, did not. It is unlikely that their original plans included joining a revolution. They returned to Tennessee while Crockett's nephew William Patton did enlist, as did a number of other Tennesseans. One, Micajah Autry, a lawyer from Jackson, Tennessee, closed a letter to his wife on January 13 with the postscript, "Col. Crockett has just joined our company."

After enlisting he formed a small group into a mounted

"spy" or scout company, such as the one he had joined during the Creek War, and headed into the Texas interior. By January 23, the company reached Washington-on-the-Brazos, southwest of Nacogdoches. There, he signed an IOU in the amount of $7.50 for accommodations for himself, four others, and their horses, the last record of his journey in his handwriting.

It is uncertain if he left Nacogdoches under any specific orders since the nascent Texan government and army were disorganized and a number of factions were fighting for control of both. His exact route is also subject to debate, he and his men meandering about the countryside before reaching San Antonio de Béxar.

After General Cos's force was driven from San Antonio in December, the Texans garrisoned the town under the command of James Clinton Neill, a native of North Carolina who had come to Texas in 1831. Instrumental in the fight for the Gonzales cannon in the fall, and in the battle of Béxar, Neill held the rank of lieutenant colonel of artillery. His garrison consisted of a staff, an artillery company, and one or two small infantry companies, which, in the manner of all loosely organized volunteer forces, dwindled in number as boredom and the need to care for families and homesteads grew. Beginning in early January he sent out a series of urgent requests to Texan officials describing the appalling weakness of his post, and requesting men, supplies, and ammunition. He knew that when Mexico sent an army to reclaim its territory, San Antonio, the most important town in the region and the scene of their recent defeat and humiliation, would be its main objective.

Crockett and his men may have been dispatched in response to Neill's requests for aid, or they may have gone to San Antonio de Béxar on their own, knowing that a need for men existed there. All that is certain is that Crockett and his company reached the town at some point between February 5 and 10. Years later, Antonio Menchaca, a prominent San Antonian, reported making the initial contact with Crockett and fourteen young men who accompanied him as the volunteers picked their way through an old cemetery on San Pedro Creek, west of the town. As usual, the Tennessean's arrival attracted attention, and on February 10, the garrison threw a party in his honor.

Other reinforcements had answered Neill's calls for assistance before Crockett and his men arrived. On January 18, James Bowie led a volunteer force into San Antonio, followed two weeks later by William Barret Travis with a small company of regular cavalry. Bowie, a forty-year-old Kentuckian, had emigrated to Texas from Louisiana in 1828 and married into the prominent Verimendi family of San Antonio, then lost his wife and in-laws in the cholera epidemic of 1833. Now he had returned at the request of Sam Houston to reinforce Neill as well as assess the situation there. Sam Houston, the former governor of Tennessee, a close friend of Andrew Jackson's, and rising as the leading military figure of Texas, had directed Bowie to destroy the fortifications in the town—meaning those in the military plaza. With Bowie under orders, Houston wrote a letter to Governor Henry Smith, the civil leader among the Texans, advancing the possibility of abandoning San Antonio altogether, removing the artillery, and destroying the Alamo. But Bowie, with emotional and financial ties to the town, determined that it must be held. On February 2, he wrote to Governor Smith, "Col. Neill & Myself have come to the solemn resolution that we will rather die in these ditches than give it up to the enemy."

Twenty-six-year-old Travis, a South Carolinian raised in

Alabama, had moved to Texas in 1831. At the outbreak of hostilities in the fall, he set aside his law practice in San Felipe and eagerly joined the newly forming army, since for the past four years he had been one of the leading voices calling for defiance of Mexican authority. He held the rank of lieutenant colonel in the Texan cavalry but for all his passion for revolution, he rode to the relief of Neill reluctantly. As a high-ranking cavalry officer he could not see the logic in Governor Smith's orders, assigning him to a fortified defensive position instead of allowing him to dash about the countryside on horseback, in keeping with the chivalric image he held of himself. He traveled with his slave and servant, a man named Joe, and thirty cavalrymen under Captain John Hubbard Forsyth, a physician from Avon, New York. The proud and moody Travis wrote to Governor Smith, "I am unwilling to risk my reputation (which is ever dear to a soldier) by going off into the enemies' country with such little means, so few men, & them so badly equipped." He felt so strongly about this that he threatened to resign his commission if his orders were not rescinded. When they were not, he could not bring himself to disobey them and continued on, arriving in San Antonio on February 2. A few days later, Crockett and the men who rode with him also joined the garrison, which now comprised a number of small, disparate units, all with loyalty to their individual leaders.

During the party in Crockett's honor, a scout sent out earlier by the Texans returned to San Antonio and reported a strong Mexican army, under Santa Anna himself, preparing to cross the Rio Grande into Texas. The men receiving this intelligence, among them Travis, Bowie, and Crockett, reasoned that since it would take a large force almost two weeks to cross the prairie from the Rio Grande to San Antonio, the welcoming party might as well continue.

News of the approaching enemy force did not galvanize the Texans to any concerted action, and events of the next few days almost saved Santa Anna the trouble of taking the town. On February 11, Green B. Jameson, a lawyer from Kentucky who served as Colonel Neill's engineering officer, reported in a letter that many of the volunteers in San Antonio were leaving that day since they had been in the field for two months without any pay, clothing, or provisions. He mentioned Crockett's presence along with that of Bowie and Travis, and wrote that two "staunch independence men" had been elected to represent the garrison at the constitutional convention. Last, he reported that Colonel Neill had been called away from his command due to illness in his family, causing great regret among the men, but that Neill promised to return within twenty days.

Neill's appointment of Travis, the highest-ranking regular army officer present, as temporary commander of the San Antonio garrison caused a problem among the volunteer troops. By custom, volunteers elected their own officers, just as those under Neill had elected him in December. As commander of the post, he had both volunteer and regular troops under his authority, but when he appointed Travis to take his place pending his return, the volunteers objected, demanding the right to vote for their own leader. With Neill gone, Travis acceded to their demands, allowing an election with the assumption that in any event, the officer chosen would be a subordinate.

The volunteers elected the popular Jim Bowie, who, after celebrating to drunkenness, assumed authority over the entire garrison as well as the town, preventing local families from departing with their carts filled with their belongings, and releasing both military and civil prisoners for work details. Travis tried to regain some control but without success, and for a brief time pulled his regulars, and a volunteer company that had chosen to serve under him, out of town to the southwest to camp on the Medina River.

Crockett knew intimately the system of popular election of officers by volunteer troops, but it is unknown if he played any role in the controversy, or whose leadership he supported. The political bickering of Washington paled by comparison to the San Antonio dispute, playing out with the reappearance of the enemy only days away. It took Colonel Neill, riding back to San Antonio with supplies he had purchased for the post, to settle the rift. By February 14, an understanding had been reached that Travis would command the regulars and volunteer cavalry, Bowie all other volunteers, and they would sign all correspondence and general orders together until Neill, who had continued on his mission, returned. With the controversy over, the garrison had little to do but hope for additional reinforcements and wait for the arrival of the Mexican army.

On the afternoon of February 23, the vanguard of the Mexican force, with Santa Anna leading it, appeared on the outskirts of San Antonio. An attempt to catch the Texans unaware early that morning failed when a cavalry force sent forward halted and took up a defensive position after receiving reports that the Texans were about to attack it. By the time Santa Anna discovered the delay, he had lost any element of surprise. Travis and Bowie, seeing the enemy's approach, abandoned the town proper, moving all their men to the east side of the San Antonio River and into the questionable security of the former mission, San Antonio de Valero, popularly known as the Alamo.

At three-thirty that afternoon, Santa Anna and his troops took possession of San Antonio with little resistance. With Travis's men fortified in the Alamo, the generalissimo had no choice but to besiege the mission until its defenders surrendered, or until enough of his army caught up with him to take the position by assault. Within the hour both sides established the terms of the conflict: Santa Anna ordered a red flag, indicating no quarter, hoisted on the bell tower of the San Fernando church in the middle of town; the Texans fired a cannon in defiance of that merciless symbol. Later, someone informed Bowie that the Mexicans had called for a parley before the cannon had been fired, prompting him to send the Alamo's engineer, Green Jameson, with a flag of truce to ascertain if this was the case. Santa Anna's aide-de-camp rebuffed Jameson, telling the messenger that the Mexican army could not come to terms under any conditions with rebellious foreigners, who, if they wished to save their lives, could only do so by surrendering immediately.

Upon Jameson's return to the Alamo with the news, Travis sent a messenger of his own to speak to Santa Anna's top aide, Colonel Juan Nepomuceno Almonte, a renowned, educated officer who had toured the United States and Texas two years earlier. Travis sent word that if Almonte wished to parley, he would receive him with much pleasure. Almonte answered that it did not become the Mexican government to make any proposition through him, and that he only had permission to hear the propositions of the rebels. The time for possible truces and negotiations had passed with the first cannon shot.

The Alamo

Fate intervened in the question of the command of the Alamo.

At some point during the first day of the siege an unidentified illness incapacitated Bowie, leaving the sole authority for the garrison and fort to Travis. Crockett, who held no command within the grounds other than that over his own small scout company, remained in the background, pitching in whenever needed.

He had come to Texas for a new start and to explore the endless possibilities of the vast lands above the Rio Grande. In order to earn these things he had allowed himself to be confined to one small area within the crumbling limestone walls of the Alamo, parts of which were ninety years old. The former mission, a three-acre complex of walls and buildings, had the shape of a capital *L*. Its main plaza ran north and south, comprising the vertical axis of the L, with a series of small rooms built on the interior of its west wall. Sturdier two-story buildings, known as the "long barracks," stood across the main plaza on the east side. A freestanding north wall, shored up with earth and timber, formed the top of the L, an exposed and vulnerable position. A building known as the "low barracks," pierced by the main entrance and protected on the outside by a timber and earthen fortification, formed the south wall of the main plaza. A small courtyard opened to the east of the main gate, along the lower axis of the L, and to the east of that stood the Alamo's most recognizable building, its roofless church, facing west. A wooden palisade ran from the southwest corner of the church to the low barracks, enclosing the small courtyard from the outside. The walls of the church were twenty-two feet high, those of the rest of the mission only eight to twelve feet high, with the west wall facing the edge of the town, one-quarter mile away across the river.

Travis had only 150 men to defend the Alamo, and as of the first day of the siege his garrison was outnumbered ten to one. Luckily, the Texans had been able to drive a small herd of cattle into the compound, and bring in about ninety bushels of corn liberated from nearby houses. Water flowed into the fort through an irrigation ditch, but wells were dug in case Santa Anna's men cut off the supply. In addition to the Texan soldiers, a number of noncombatant women and children, family members of defenders, and a handful of slaves belonging to some of the men, took refuge within the walls when the Mexican army appeared.

Santa Anna began the process of besieging the Alamo by ordering artillery positions set up, and cutting off access to and from the fort as more of his troops arrived. Travis sent out the first of a number of dispatches keeping the rest of Texas informed of his plight, calling for assistance while hoping to hold the Mexicans in position until reinforcements rallied to him.

With dramatic flair, he wrote a message on February 24, the second day of the siege, addressed to "the People of Texas and all Americans in the world." He reported on the strength of the enemy army, and of the cannonade he and his men had endured for the last twenty-four hours. He wrote of Santa Anna's demand for surrender, but declared that he would "never surrender or retreat," expressing his determination to "die like a soldier who never forgets what is due to his own honor and that of his country."

At 10 A.M. on February 25, the Mexican general sent nearly three hundred men in an exploratory attack against the Alamo's walls. Travis wrote that his men conducted themselves with firmness and bravery during the two-hour action, singling out two who sallied forth under fire to torch some houses providing cover for the enemy. He praised several other men, including Crockett, who "was seen at all points animating the men to do their duty." After this initial action the tedium of the siege set in for the defenders, who had little to do other than dodge cannonballs, shore up defenses, and watch the Mexican army increase in strength every day.

Among the noncombatants within the walls was the family of Gregorio Esparza, a local Tejano—a Texan of Mexican descent—who had thrown in his lot with the rebels. He entered the fort after sunset on the first day of the siege with his wife, Anna, eight-year-old son, Enrique, and his other children. Later in his life Enrique gave a number of interviews describing the siege and battle. He recalled Crockett's arrival in San Antonio, describing him as wearing a buckskin suit and a coonskin cap, a man, he said, who "made everybody laugh and forget their worries."

"I remember Crockett," he stated. "He was a tall, slim man, with black whiskers. He was always at the head. The Mexicans called him Don Benito. The Americans said he was Crockett. He would often come to the fire and warm his hands and say a few words to us in the Spanish language."

In a later interview he described the Tennessean as "the leading spirit . . . He was everywhere. He went to every exposed point and personally directed the fighting. Travis was chief in command, but he depended more upon the judgment of Crockett and that brave man's intrepidity than upon his own."

Crockett's forty-nine years made him one of the elders among the Alamo defenders. His status as a national celebrity and his good humor ensured a place for him as a natural, if not official leader within the garrison. It is likely that many of the younger men felt confident, despite their perilous situation, with his presence and that of Bowie, each man with heroic reputations.

When Crockett formed his scout company he probably expected to fulfill the same duties as assigned to him in the Creek War: riding ahead of the main army, locating the enemy, bagging game when the opportunity presented itself, and generally freelancing. But such services were impossible within the walls of the Alamo, which began to resemble a death trap to its defenders. By March 3, Travis reported that the enemy had kept up a continuous bombardment for eight days with two howitzers and two long nine-pound cannon throwing two hundred shells within the fort. The Mexicans had established entrenched encampments on all sides: eight hundred yards north, eight hundred yards northeast, three hundred yards south, and four hundred yards west, within San Antonio itself. He stated that no man had been injured despite the intense shelling and that spirits were still high.

As serious as the situation had become, the defenders' position was not hopeless. Couriers had gone out carrying requests for reinforcements, and the prospects for their success were believed to be good. Crockett always retained implicit faith in the tradition of volunteer citizen-soldiers who rose to the occasion when called upon. His father had succeeded with the "over the mountain men" at Kings Mountain, as he had with the Tennessee volunteers during the Creek War. Faith in this system had been validated already on March 1, when thirty-two men from the town of Gonzales made their way through the Mexican lines to reinforce the Alamo.

On March 2, Texan officials met at the town of Washington-on-the-Brazos, declaring themselves independent of Mexico and framing a constitution and government. Two years earlier Crockett had stood on Bunker Hill and pledged to "go for my country always and everywhere." Texas had become his country now, but its shaky independence still had to be secured.

Although confined in the Alamo, he had no shortage of friends about him with whom he could reminisce about home, or the old days of law and politics. The majority of Alamo defenders were Tennesseans, and in their predicament it did not matter much whether one was a Jackson man or not. Micajah Autry, who had enlisted with Crockett in Nacogdoches, now belonged to the garrison along with his group of companions, a number of them young lawyers like himself. Almeron Dickinson, a twenty-six-year-old blacksmith from Hardeman County, Tennessee, who now lived in Gonzales, served as one of the Alamo's artillery officers. His wife, Susannah, also from Tennessee, and their fifteen-month-old daughter were with him in San Antonio when the Mexican army arrived, and took refuge in the fort.

Despite the hope the defenders had for reinforcements, Crockett became restless during the siege. Susannah Dickinson stated years later that she heard him repeat a number of times, "I think we had better march out and die in the open air. I don't like to be hemmed up."

March 3 brought no reinforcements but Travis received some encouraging news. Lieutenant James Butler Bonham, a courier whom Travis had sent to Gonzales, returned with a message from Robert M. Williamson, a lawyer, newspaperman, and close friend now serving as the commander of the Texas Ranging Corps, a mounted military force and forerunner of the Texas Rangers. In his letter dated March 1, Williamson urged the Alamo commander to sustain himself until others were able to come to his assistance, assuring him that sixty men had left Gonzales for the Alamo and should be there by the time Travis received his message. He further stated that Colonel James W. Fannin had started out from the town of Goliad, ninety miles southeast of San Antonio, three days earlier with three hundred men and four artillery pieces, and that another three hundred men were expected to assemble at Gonzales from neighboring towns. Travis already had received some of those men, the thirty-two from Gonzales and, according to Williamson, could count on another 630. Even if those reinforcements were not able to join the defenders inside the Alamo, they could certainly break the siege outside by creating a second front for Santa Anna to deal with.

While the men of the Alamo received rumors of reinforcements, Santa Anna received the real thing. In the late afternoon of March 3, the Mexican army's Aldama and Toluca battalions, and its battalion of combat engineers, the Zapadores, entered San Antonio after an exhausting forced march. Now the generalissimo had the troops needed to take the Alamo by storm. That night, Travis gave the restless Crockett the opportunity to fulfill his role as scout. The defenders needed the reinforcements with Colonel Fannin in Goliad. Travis had sent express riders to the colonel several times calling for his assistance. But Fannin, a Georgian who had attended the United States Military Academy, had made two halfhearted attempts to reach the Alamo, only to give up when some of his wagons broke down or his oxen wandered away. He had limped back to his own fort, the Presidio la Bahía at Goliad, to wait in indecision for orders from a superior, or the appearance of the Mexican army, to move him to action.

Crockett and two other men left the Alamo on the night of March 3, traveling twenty miles east to the Cibolo crossing on the Gonzales–San Antonio road, trying to make contact with Fannin's men and lead them back to the Alamo. They did not know that the Goliad force had given up its relief attempts, but did encounter fifty men from a number of small units trying to reach the fort. Crockett and one of his scouts led the group back to the Alamo, sending the third man on to Gonzales with dispatches.

Once outside the walls of the fort, Crockett had choices. He could have ridden on to Gonzales himself, but stubbornness and single-mindedness were indelible in his character, and he chose to return to the lethal confinement of the Alamo, leading the men he had encountered on the Cibolo.

Colonel Almonte later recorded in his diary that a group of

Texans from the Alamo attacked Mexican forces that night but were repulsed. He had mistaken Crockett and the men with him, cutting their way back into the fort, as a maneuver originating from inside the mission.

On March 4, Santa Anna held a meeting of his chief officers at which a debate developed over whether he should send his men against the Alamo walls, or await the arrival of some expected artillery pieces to further soften up the defenses. The general listened to his officers but while he reserved making a decision, he did order a battery moved to cover the vulnerable north wall of the Alamo in preparation for an attack.

By the following day, the generalissimo had decided not to await the artillery. He may have felt confident that the reinforcements he had just received were capable of handling the assignment, or his patience may simply have run out. If one group of rebels had gotten through his lines to the fort, then others might succeed as well. He decided to put an end to the debilitating siege.

At two o'clock on Saturday afternoon, March 5, 1836, he issued the battle orders, specifying four attack columns, the units to comprise each, and the officers who would command them in the attack the following morning. He designated three of the columns to assault the exposed north wall in a pincer movement, and the smaller fourth column, in a diversionary move, to attack the wooden palisade on the south side. Cavalry and lancers would patrol the area around the Alamo to prevent any defender's escape. He issued twenty-six scaling ladders to the north columns, as well as four crowbars and axes to be used against the wood shoring of the wall or any doors in the wall, and two ladders to the south column. The general wanted only experienced men for the battle, ordering all raw recruits to remain in camp. The columns were to begin moving into position at 2 A.M. He ordered all of his soldiers to have their weapons, "especially bayonets," in top condition.

The question of what to do with any defenders surrendering or taken alive required no explanation. Santa Anna had established that policy on the first day of the siege when he had the red flag flown from the San Fernando church. If that had not made his message clear enough, he had put it in writing to his cavalry commander, General Joaquín Ramírez y Sesma, on February 29, instructing Sesma to intercept the expected reinforcements to the Alamo from Goliad. In closing the orders he reminded his general, "In this war you know there are no prisoners."

Like a Hero

Santa Anna's plan called for the assault on the Alamo to begin at 4:30 A.M., March 6, but the complexity of moving, positioning, and coordinating an attack of nearly fifteen hundred men caused a delay. He may have intentionally pushed the time back so his men would benefit by some feeble daylight while entering the hostile compound.

The Mexican cannonade ceased during the evening of March 5 while the troops prepared to move into battle position. The Texans did not get a chance to rest with the respite in the shelling, working long into the night strengthening their defenses.

Travis had only settled into his bunk in the headquarters of the Alamo after making his rounds in the early morning hours when the post's adjutant, Captain John J. Baugh of Virginia, burst into the room. "Colonel Travis, the Mexicans are coming!" he yelled. The colonel bolted from his cot, grabbing his double-barreled shotgun and sword, and calling to his slave, Joe, to follow him. Joe, taking his own rifle, rushed with him into the dawn and the growing din of battle at the north wall.

It is not known where Crockett was stationed at this moment or to what area of the fort he had been assigned. It is likely that he was near the church, where the noncombatants were quartered, since Enrique Esparza remembered seeing him there. "Crockett was one of the few who were wide awake when the final crisis and crash came," he said.

Travis and Joe reached the north wall as the rest of the garrison came to life and the Alamo erupted in cannon and small-arms fire. The Texan commander had just enough time to yell some encouragement to his men—"Come on, boys, the Mexicans are upon us, and we'll give them hell!" He aimed his shotgun over the wall but only managed to fire once before being struck by Mexican bullets and tumbling onto the earthen artillery ramp.

Santa Anna's columns struck the exposed north wall in the prescribed pincer movement, enduring punishing fire from within the fort. He had intended his advance to be rapid and silent so that his force would reach the walls before the Texans could respond. However, one unit, caught up in the excitement of the moment, raised a noisy cheer for their general and the Mexican Republic, eliminating any chance for surprise.

Fire from the fort brought down Colonel Francisco Duque, leading the column on the north side, with a severe wound, causing his men to falter momentarily. At the same time the Alamo defenders drove the Mexicans attacking the northeast corner to their right, forcing them to merge with the north column. General Cos, who had been ordered back to Texas by Santa Anna, fared no better with his column to the northwest. His men veered to their left in the storm of gunfire, adding to the chaos of the other columns. The commanding general, at the artillery battery to the north, saw his columns in a jumbled mass and feared his entire attack was in danger of stalling. He reluctantly committed his reserve units, the grenadier companies of each battalion, which he had held out of the original plans, and his combat engineers, the Zapadores.

With Colonel Duque wounded, one of his aides, Lieutenant José Enrique de la Peña, an officer with a troubled career, had a chance to prove himself. Although he held an official rank of captain of cavalry, the Mexican military saw fit not to use him in that capacity in the Texan campaign. In the months before Santa Anna marched north, De la Peña had preoccupied himself with making a number of urgent requests to be assigned legation duty in Europe in the rank of lieutenant colonel, which he felt he deserved. Instead, his superiors ordered him north, with the rank of lieutenant, and he arrived with Duque only two days earlier.

De la Peña rushed to the rear to summon General Manuel Fernandez Castrillón, leading the rear guard of Duque's force, to take over the column. While Castrillón moved forward, assumed command, and restored some order and discipline to the attack, De la Peña ran across the front of the attack several times delivering important messages.

The fresh units launched themselves into the confused tangle at the north wall, giving the already overtaxed defenders more to handle. By sheer weight of numbers the Mexican reserves and the men from the original columns began clambering up the scaling ladders and the uneven timbers bracing the outside of the wall. On the south, the diversionary column veered from its original target, the wooden palisade connecting the church and low barracks, bypassed the outerworks protecting the main gate, and struck the southwest corner of the fort.

These men, a hundred in number, struggled up their two ladders, overcoming the Texan artillery crew in that position. With footholds at opposite ends of the Alamo, Mexican soldiers were able to surmount the walls unimpeded, flowing over, as one survivor described them, "like sheep."

Since the beginning of the siege, Travis and his men had hoped to hold the Mexican force in check until reinforcements reached them, but, with the Texan commander dead, and Mexican soldiers pouring over the walls in increasing numbers, the Alamo ceased to be either a fortress or a rallying point for the Texas army. Now it became nothing more than a killing ground.

Santa Anna's troops fanned out through the compound, turning captured cannon against the defenders, resorting to the bayonet when the action moved too swiftly for them to reload their cumbersome Brown Bess muskets. Texans on the walls, with the enemy closing in on them from both sides, made split-second, life-or-death decisions. Some jumped from the walls to seek cover in rooms or buildings within the compound, others jumped outside for a chance at survival in the countryside. At least three groups of Texans chose the latter course: one leaving on the east side, another from the south, and the last from the west side of the fort. General Sesma, commanding the cavalry around the Alamo, reported that the Texans did not flee in blind panic but "marched with organization to the plain trying to avail themselves of adjoining brush country." Lancers charged to intercept each group, trapping and cutting them down in ditches outside the fort. One fleeing defender, armed with a double-barreled shotgun and pistol, managed to kill a Mexican corporal before being skewered on a lance. Another, concealed under a bush, had to be shot when he could not be flushed out to the waiting lances, and another was killed after hiding under the bridge crossing the San Antonio River. Years later, Maria de Jesús Buquor of San Antonio reported that she saw seven Texans make it as far as the river before being shot or sabered on the bank.

Inside the Alamo, Mexican infantrymen cleared each building and room, killing any man they found, including the sick and wounded. Jim Bowie had been out of action during the entire siege due to his illness and it is generally agreed that the Mexicans killed him while he lay in his sickbed. The details of his death, however, as well as his location in the Alamo at the end, are subject to question. Susannah Dickinson stated that he killed two of the enemy with pistols before being sabered to death. Enrique Esparza claimed that Bowie had been placed in a small room on the north side of the church, and fired on the Mexicans with a rifle and pistols, killing one with his famous knife before he was riddled with bullets. Juana Navarro Alsbury, a cousin of Bowie's late wife, had entered the Alamo with her infant son, Alejo Pérez, Jr., and her younger sister Gertrudis Navarro, under Bowie's protection. Alsbury, a widow who had married an American doctor, Horace Alsbury, in December, later stated that she witnessed enemy soldiers carrying Bowie into the Alamo plaza, where they tossed him about on their bayonets until his blood ran down their arms and clothing. The torture continued until a Mexican cavalry officer dashed among them, lashing the soldiers with his sword, and forcing them to cease.

Travis's slave, Joe, who had taken cover in one of the rooms, fired on the enemy until his ammunition ran out. Santa Anna's soldiers had to have been aware that there were slaves, with whom they were not at war, within the Alamo, since after the gunshots had died down a Mexican officer appeared at the room's door, calling out in English, "Are there any Negroes here?" Joe stepped out from concealment and answered, "Yes, here's one." This response startled two soldiers, one of whom fired, slightly wounding him, while the other nicked him with a bayonet. Only the intervention of the officer, who beat the soldiers back with the flat of his sword, saved Joe's life.

For the most part, the action within the walls moved too quickly and furiously for any defender to attempt to surrender or to expect mercy if he tried. Juana Alsbury and her sister were sheltered in a room separate from the other noncombatants. She was comforted only by knowing that her husband had been sent on a scouting mission before the Mexican army arrived, and was not present during the battle. When she realized that the Texans were being overwhelmed she asked her sister to open the door of their room to show the Mexican soldiers that only women and children were inside. When the soldiers stormed into the room, a Texan named Mitchell, who had been ill, ran to protect her and she watched in horror as the soldiers bayoneted him to death by her side. Other Mexicans pursued a young Tejano defender into her room, stabbing him with bayonets then firing into his lifeless body.

Most of the noncombatants endured the battle within the walls of the church, the Alamo's sturdiest building. There, Susannah Dickinson remembered sixteen-year-old Galba Fuqua, a neighbor of hers from the town of Gonzales, run into her room with his jaw broken by a bullet and blood flowing from his mouth. He tried to tell her something but could not make himself understood, even while holding his jaws together with his hands. Finally, he gave up, shaking his head and running back to rejoin his comrades.

She believed the fight had raged for two hours before her husband, Almeron, rushed to her exclaiming, "Great God, Sue, the Mexicans are inside our walls! All is lost! If they spare you, save my child." He kissed her, drew his sword, and plunged back into the fight. She did not see him again until Mexican soldiers escorted her through the Alamo compound after the battle, where she witnessed soldiers plunging bayonets into the dead bodies of the Texans. She fainted when she recognized Almeron's body among them.

No one knows how Travis's trusted courier, James Butler Bonham, died. Susannah Dickinson believed that he was killed while working one of the cannons.

Enrique Esparza stated that when the Mexicans finally burst into the room where the women and children were sheltered, an American boy, not much older that himself, stood up and drew a blanket around his shoulders. In a reflex move the jumpy soldiers shot him down.

The last aggressive act by a Texan came when the garrison's thirty-six-year-old master of ordnance, Major Robert Evans, attempted to set a torch to the Alamo's gunpowder supply. When the soldiers shot him before he could set fire to the barrels, active resistance within the fort ceased, and the battle of the Alamo ended.

A room-by-room search of the compound followed in which Santa Anna's men rounded up stray noncombatants and slaves, looted property, and flushed out and finished off any surviving defenders. The general entered the fort with his staff and entourage during this cleanup operation, just as his men brought out a prisoner whom Joe described as a "little weakly body named Warner." Santa Anna ordered the man's immediate execution and the soldiers carried out the order.

Ramón Martínez Caro, a civilian secretary accompanying the generalissimo into the Alamo, reported another incident in which General Castrillón, who had taken over Colonel Duque's column during the attack, brought five survivors out into the open. Santa Anna reprimanded the general for not having killed them on the spot, and as he turned his back, his soldiers put the men to death. Dickinson said that two of the five prisoners ran to her room, where the pursuing Mexicans tortured and killed them with bayonets. In a later interview, she described three unarmed defenders she believed were artillerymen, being shot down in her presence.

Crockett probably died in the courtyard in front of the Alamo church. Susannah Dickinson saw his body in that area. "I recognized Colonel Crockett lying dead and mutilated between the church and the two-story barrack building, and even remember seeing his peculiar cap lying by his side," she was quoted as saying.

Enrique Esparza stated that Crockett "was everywhere during the siege and personally slew many of the enemy with his rifle, his pistol and his knife. He fought to his last breath. He fell immediately in front of the large double doors which he defended with the force that was by his side. . . . When he died there was a heap of slain in front and on each side of him. These he had killed before he finally fell on top of the heap."

Eualia Yorba, a young woman protecting her children at the time of the battle, had taken refuge in the house of a San Antonio priest, where she witnessed the battle. When the firing and cries had died down at about 9 A.M., a Mexican colonel appeared at the house requesting the priest proceed to the Alamo to comfort Santa Anna's wounded and dying. Yorba accompanied the priest, entering the scene of carnage, and providing aid for the maimed and moaning men. She remembered seeing Crockett, whom she knew from his time in San Antonio before the siege. She said, "He lay dead by the side of a dying man, whose bloody and powder-stained face I was washing. Colonel Crockett was about fifty years old at that time. His coat and rough woolen shirt were soaked with blood so that the original color was hidden, for the eccentric hero must have died of some ball in the chest or a bayonet thrust."

According to Travis's slave, Crockett and a few of the men who entered the Alamo with him were found lying together with twenty-one of the enemy dead around them. Santa Anna had become aware of Crockett's presence as one of the leading figures of the garrison during the course of the siege. It is unlikely that the general would have known of the Tennessean as a congressman or of his prominence in the United States. Joe never mentioned it, but Susannah Dickinson later said that Santa Anna had Joe point out Crockett's body along with that of Travis. In his victory report to the Mexican government, the generalissimo wrote, "Among the corpses are those of Bowie and Travis, who styled themselves Colonels, and also that of Crockett, and several leading men."

Santa Anna had the bodies of the Texans removed to a stand of trees called the Alameda, a short distance to the southeast of the fort, where his soldiers and civilians from town stacked the bodies and piled wood on them. In the early evening the ghastly pyres were ignited, burning for two days and consuming the remains of the defenders of the Alamo.

"No More to Be Seen in the Walks of Men"

Two Tejano scouts, Anselmo Vargara and Andrés Bárcinas, brought the first news of the Alamo battle to Sam Houston on March 11. They had not witnessed the fight but had received the information from a trusted friend. In Gonzales two days later, Houston sent out his valued scout, Erastus Smith, with two others to range toward San Antonio and ascertain the truth. They returned before dark with a distraught Susannah Dickinson, her daughter, and Travis's slave confirming the Texan commander's worst fears and spreading anguish and panic among the citizens of the town. Some of the Gonzales men had been part of the original garrison under Neill, many others had ridden to their aid, and now all were feared lost. The news also set in motion what would become known as the "Runaway Scrape" in which Texan civilians, and Houston's untrained army, reeled eastward before the Mexican advance in a dangerous cat-and-mouse game. Houston, employing a scorched-earth policy, ordered Gonzales burned as the Texans moved out.

Even before he had received verification from Susannah Dickinson, Houston believed that the Alamo had fallen and its defenders killed. He dispatched letters on March 11 describing the battle based on the intelligence received from the scouts Vargara and Bárcinas, writing in one, "All within the Fort perished. Seven of them were killed by order of Santa Anna when in the act of giving up their arms," and in the other, "After the fort was carried, seven men surrendered. . . . They were murdered by his [Santa Anna's] orders." Since Houston's intelligence on the battle derived from a witness outside the fort, the seven men he described as executed were likely the same ones Maria de Jesús Buquor saw killed on the riverbank.

By March 15, the dreaded news had reached Benjamin Briggs Goodrich, a physician and signer of the Texas Declaration of Independence, in Washington-on-the-Brazos. Goodrich passed on what he had learned in a letter, stating, "Seven of our brave men, being all that were left alive, called for quarter and to see Santa Anna, but were instantly shot by order of the fiendish tyrant." He added, "Col. Bowie was murdered in his sick bed. Among the number of your acquaintances, murdered in the Alamo, were Col. David Crockett, Micajah Autry, formerly of Haysborough, John Hays, son of Andrew Hays of Nashville, and my unfortunate brother John C. Goodrich."

While Goodrich cited seven men executed, reflecting the intelligence Houston had received, he identified five acquaintances who had died in the battle, describing them as having been "murdered." The proximity of these two bits of information in his letter gave the impression that those he specifically named were five of the seven executed. This became the seed for the later reports of Crockett having been killed after the battle.

On March 19 the schooner *Comanche* departed Washington-on-the-Brazos bound for New Orleans carrying news of the Alamo disaster. In New Orleans, newspapers eagerly picked up and published the story. The *Louisiana Advertiser* reported, "The Alamo has fallen into the hands of the Mexicans under Santa Anna, and its garrison have been massacred in cold blood after their arms were surrendered. Col. David Crockett is among the slain." The article stated that the entire garrison was killed after surrendering and that Crockett "fell fighting like a tiger." The *New Orleans True American* reported, "The Mexicans fought desperately until daylight, when seven only of the garrison were found alive. We regret to say that Col. David Crockett and his companion Mr. Benton, also Col. Bonham of South Carolina, were of the number who cried for quarter but were told there was no mercy for them. They then continued fighting until the whole were butchered."

While the news of Crockett's death spread through New Orleans, the *Morning Courier and New York Enquirer* of March 26 amazingly reported his survival, stating, "Colonel Crockett, as we said when we announced the rumor of his death, is *not* dead, but still alive and grinning." In New York the *Monroe Democrat* picked up the story, adding, "Davy Crockett not dead—We are happy to state on the authority of a letter from Tennessee that the report of the eccentric Davy Crockett is not true. 'He started (says the letter) on a hunting expedition to the Rocky Mountains, and then dropped down into Texas; but we expect him home early in the Spring.'" Ironically, both newspapers sought to correct reports published in February when it was thought that he and his companions had been killed by Indians during their east Texas hunting expedition.

Crockett's family received the devastating news in mid-April, his daughter Matilda stating, "We were all greatly distressed when we heard that he had been killed; we could hardly believe it." The family's reaction was not surprising considering that they all had received rumors of his death before, and he had always reappeared. Their hopes for his survival may also have been raised by other newspaper accounts, such as one headlined in the *Cincinnati Whig*, "COLONEL CROCKETT, the hero and patriot it is said IS NOT DEAD!!" The story described him as having been discovered covered with wounds in the Alamo after the Mexicans had abandoned it, and then taken to a nearby home to recover. The paper, while voicing its doubts about the rumor, expressed its hope that the story would prove authentic.

During this period of uncertainty, Elizabeth Crockett received a package and letter from Isaac Jones, with whom her husband had swapped watches at Lost Prairie, Arkansas. The package contained Crockett's inscribed watch, with a letter describing the circumstances of the exchange. In expressing his condolences at the hero's death Jones wrote: "In his loss Freedom has been deprived of one of her bravest sons, in whose bosom universal philanthropy glowed with as genial warmth as ever animated the heart of an American citizen. When he fell, a soldier died. To bemoan his fate, is to pay a tribute of grateful respect to Nature—he seemed to be her son."

While America adjusted to the idea of Crockett's death, Texas fought for its existence. Following the fall of the Alamo, the Mexican army swept eastward in three wings, driving the Texan army and settlers before it. General Antonio Gaona commanded the force to the north, General José Cosme de Urrea the force to the south, and Santa Anna the center.

On March 14, Houston ordered Colonel Fannin at Goliad to blow up his Presidio la Bahía and remove all of his men and any artillery he could transport to the town of Guadalupe Victoria. Fannin delayed until March 19, finally departing with his men, nine cannon, and about one thousand muskets, but insufficient food and water. After spending too much time recovering a lost cannon from the San Antonio River, then allowing hungry oxen to wander about grazing, he was overtaken by General Urrea's force. Caught in the open, he formed his men into a hollow square from which they repelled three Mexican attacks by sundown, but surrendered the following day due to a scarcity of ammunition, food, and water. One week later, despite Urrea's recommendation for mercy, Fannin and more than three hundred of his men were executed by order of Santa Anna.

The generalissimo's column pursued the Texan force eastward until they reached the San Jacinto River and Buffalo Bayou, about twenty miles east of modern-day Houston. There, on April 20, a Texan cavalry unit skirmished with Mexican troops, coming close to bringing on a full-scale battle. Both sides withdrew from the field that afternoon and set up camps a scant three-quarters of a mile apart.

The next morning, General Cos joined Santa Anna's column with 540 men, swelling its ranks to 1,200. In the Texan camp, Houston ordered his eight hundred volunteers into battle formation while he and his officers held a council of war. While the Texans debated, the Mexican force lapsed into complacency, with soldiers lounging behind a breastwork of baggage, saddles, and equipment, and with Santa Anna retiring to his tent, leaving General Castrillón in charge of the army.

Between three-thirty and four in the afternoon of April 21,

1836, Houston made his move, leading his men across an open field toward the Mexican camp. By the time Santa Anna and his men realized they were under attack, it was too late for them to rally. In less than twenty minutes the Texan line swept up and over the barricade, routing the enemy, and killing or capturing most of the Mexican force, including Santa Anna, who was taken prisoner the following day.

Other Mexican forces remained in the field in Texas, but with the destruction of Santa Anna's column and his capture, the revolution ended with Texas on its way toward independence.

If the Crockett family held out any hope that David had survived the Alamo, they abandoned it by the summer. John Wesley Crockett, in a letter dated July 9, 1836, wrote: "You have doubtless seen the account of my father's fall at the Alamo in Texas. He is gone from among us, and is no more to be seen in the walks of men, but in his death, like Sampson, he slew more of his enemies than in all his life. Even his most bitter enemies here, I believe, have buried all animosity, and joined the general lamentation over his untimely end."

On the same day that the son wrote his letter, a story appeared in the *Morning Courier and New York Enquirer* reporting that Crockett had been one of six Americans discovered near a wall, "yet unconquered," in the Alamo. Surrounded, and ordered to surrender by General Castrillón, the six men did so with his promise of protection, "finding resistance any longer in vain—indeed, perfect madness." The article described Castrillón bringing his prisoners to Santa Anna, asking how he should dispose of them, and causing the generalissimo to fly into a violent rage.

"Have I not told you before how to dispose of them? Why do you bring them to *me*?" Santa Anna said. "Murderous" and "sycophantic" Mexican officers then ran the prisoners through with their swords.

With this article, the vague stories of Crockett being executed with the whole garrison gained momentum. Readers who questioned why he was in Texas in the first place could reason that since he voluntarily cast his lot with the rebels, challenging the armed might of Mexico, he paid the price for his decision. However, the kindly, fun-loving Crockett *murdered* at the order of a fiendish Mexican general painted an entirely different picture. America already mourned his loss, with men and women weeping on the streets of Nashville, and now newspapers like the *Natchez Courier* were lamenting, "Poor Davey Crockett, the quaint, the laughter-moving, but fearless upright Crockett, to be butchered by such a wretch as Santa Anna—is not to be borne!"

The "witness" who related the story of the Texans' execution and the reporter who wrote the first report specifically identifying Crockett as one of a small group executed at the Alamo were never identified. Whereas other reports of the Alamo battle originated in Texas or New Orleans and spread from newspaper to newspaper north and east, this historically critical story first appeared in a New York City paper and spread southwest, to be picked up by the Richmond, Virginia, *Enquirer* on July 15, and the Frankfort, Kentucky, *Commonwealth* on July 27.

The *Morning Courier and New York Enquirer* editor, James Watson Webb, had enjoyed Crockett's company during the congressman's New York visit and accompanied him to the notorious Five Points section. As a Whig, he should have been opposed to

Andrew Jackson's vision of Manifest Destiny, for which Crockett had unknowingly sacrificed himself, but Webb was also a businessman and had become involved in land speculation in Texas. In October 1834, he helped found the New Washington Association in New York City, organized to develop a town on the Texas Gulf Coast as an agricultural and commercial center. The association's membership included a number of prominent New Yorkers as well as men from Mexico and Texas.

Members of the association had invested heavily in their Texas venture, and once the Texas revolution erupted, their only chance to capitalize on their investments hinged on Texas becoming free from Mexican rule. When the association learned that the newly organized Texas government had invalidated their land claims, it began supporting Texan annexation to the United States as a way to protect their holdings.

Once the news of San Jacinto and Santa Anna's capture reached New York, it became crucial to Webb and his partners that the Mexican general not be set free to make his way back to Mexico, there to regroup to regain Texas. One of Webb's partners wrote a series of letters to Colonel James Morgan, a Texan officer and the New Washington Association's agent in Texas, who was in charge of Mexican prisoners of war, advocating Santa Anna's execution. During the same period, Webb published the article describing Crockett's murder, painting Santa Anna as a monster and helping inflame public opinion against him.

The story in Webb's newspaper provided a time, place, and method of death of the most famous man inside the Alamo. Researchers have never been able to establish the identity of the alleged witness. The writer is suspected to have been William H. Attree, a well-known sensationalist reporter for several New

York City newspapers, including Webb's, who traveled around the United States for five months drumming up support for the Texas revolution before going to Texas himself. If the witness never existed or if the reporter exercised some poetic license in the telling, there was no harm done, especially in the opinion of those whose interest lay in the holdings of the New Washington Association, or those interested in keeping Santa Anna from regaining Texas.

Others also capitalized on Crockett's death. His publisher, Carey and Hart, had stacks of *An Account of Col. Crockett's Tour to the North and Down East*, but no market for them after the congressman's death. Then the company hit upon a solution to help move the stock. A writer named Richard Penn Smith was hired to create a Crockett "journal" describing his journey through Texas, and worked feverishly, using as source material all the books and articles on Texas that Carey and Hart could lay their hands on, and each morning delivering the new manuscript pages he had written. He peopled the work with a colorful—but fictional—group of frontier companions for Crockett, keeping the story racing along up until a last, breathless journal entry for March 5, in the Alamo: "Pop, pop, pop! Bom, bom, bom! throughout the day,—No time for memorandums now.—Go ahead!—Liberty and independence for ever!" The finished product, *Col. Crockett's Exploits and Adventures in Texas*, actually contained a number of factual elements since Smith lifted his chronology of the Alamo siege directly from the journal of Mexican Colonel Juan N. Almonte, recovered at San Jacinto and published in the *New York Herald* in June 1836. *Exploits* appeared in the summer of 1836 and became an instant success, selling out and helping clear Carey and Hart's shelves of the remaining copies of *Crockett's Tour.*

Still others, less ambitious but no less entrepreneurial, bought, sold, or possessed bits and pieces of Crockettiana. The captain of the ship *Mexico,* arriving in New York from Vera Cruz in the summer of 1836, claimed to be in possession of the hero's rifle, his shot pouch, and powder horn. However, Texas settler James W. Nichols later wrote in his journal that while in San Antonio in the late 1830s he found a Mexican in possession of Crockett's rifle, with its eighteen-pound barrel broken off at the breech. A silver plate just behind the hind sight, he said, carried the inscription "Davy Crockette."

A Crockett fiddle made an appearance in the early 1930s with affidavits from the owner that his father had bought the instrument from the hero's son Joseph in 1859. Lest anyone should doubt its authenticity, someone had written, "This fiddle is my property, Davy Crockett, Franklin County, Tenn. February 14, 1819," on the *inside* of the instrument. That Crockett did not have a son named Joseph and did not live in Franklin County in 1819 has not diminished the value, or interest in, this peculiar relic, which is proudly displayed in the Witte Museum in San Antonio today.

Another Crockett fiddle surfaced during the centennial year of the Alamo battle in the hands of an eight-year-old Texan whose father allegedly bought the instrument from a second-hand store in Mexico City in 1848. On one side of its head is carved "D. Crockett," and "Tenn., 1835, D.C., Texas, 1836" on the other.

Both fiddles are made more remarkable by the fact that in

all of his letters and autobiographical writings, Crockett never mentioned owning or playing a fiddle, nor did any of his family members. The fiddle story was first reported by Susannah Dickinson in 1875 when she was quoted as saying, "Colonel Crockett was a performer on the violin, and often during the siege took it up and played his favorite tunes." She later expanded on this, telling her granddaughter stories of Crockett playing concerts or musical competitions with Alamo defender John McGregor to see who could make the best music—or the most noise: Crockett on his fiddle or McGregor on his bagpipes. In the 1890s, Robert Hall, an early Texan settler, published his memoirs in which he identified Crockett as having played a fiddle at a frolic before leaving for Texas. This testimony, however, is not reliable, especially when the introduction of a modern edition of the memoirs cautions that readers cannot rely on everything written by Hall, describing him as part of a breed characterized as "authentic liars."

Other Crockett items have emerged, as well. A beaded vest is displayed in the modern-day Alamo as having been owned by the Tennessean, even though its beadwork appears to be of Indian tribes from a part of the country Crockett never visited. (Museum curators are said to wink and shake their heads over the vest's history.)

In the months following the Alamo battle a small herd of horses was sold around Washington, each being claimed as the one Crockett rode to Texas.

Dr. Valentine Mott of the College of Physicians and Surgeons of New York City, a leading anatomist, came away with the prize piece of Crockett memorabilia when, in his 1858 catalog of specimens, he listed as part of his collection David Crockett's skull.

Hope for a miraculous Crockett reappearance rekindled in 1840 when William C. White, an American living in Mexico, brought news to the United States that he had spoken to an American prisoner laboring in a mine in Guadalajara identifying himself as David Crockett, and asking White to forward a letter to the Crockett family in Tennessee. In Texas, the *Austin Gazette* published White's description of this meeting but not the contents of the "prisoner's" letter. White claimed to have sent the message from Matamoros, Mexico, to be mailed in New Orleans, and although he also claimed to have made a copy of the letter, he never shared its details. The *Austin Gazette* article piqued the interest of John Wesley Crockett, then a member of Congress, who had never been fully convinced of his father's death at the Alamo. He knew of the stories of Susannah Dickinson and Travis's slave identifying the body, and had heard rumors that Santa Anna, while a prisoner of the Texans, had admitted that he had ordered Crockett killed after the Tennessean's life had been spared by Colonel Almonte. But young Crockett held on to a tenuous hope that Almonte may have disobeyed Santa Anna's orders and secreted his father out of Texas, perhaps with Mexican troops returning home after the revolution.

Congressman Crockett wrote to Secretary of State John Forsyth requesting that America's minister to Mexico investigate the story, and while the envoy did so, he wrote that he had been unable to discover any further information other than a report that the "prisoner" in question had died. With that news the last hope of David Crockett's survival faded.

The Sundering

I nterest in Crockett remained strong throughout the latter half of the nineteenth century, with his memory kept alive in a variety of biographies and children's adventure books that blended details of his life with the fictions of the almanacs, *Sketches and Eccentricities,* and *Exploits and Adventures in Texas.* In 1872, a play, *Davey Crockett; or, Be Sure You're Right, Then Go Ahead,* starred noted character actor Frank Mayo as the hero. By 1877 it had been performed a thousand times, closing after a nineteen-year run due to the death of its star.

The Tennessean's reputation suffered a serious blow in 1927 when Harvard-educated and Pulitzer prize–winning historian Vernon Louis Parrington published his *Main Currents in American Thought.* In this work he portrayed the hero to the world as a "sloven . . . a true frontier wastrel . . . the biggest frog in a very small puddle, first among the Smart Alecks of the canebrakes," and credited Crockett's own *A Narrative of the Life of David*

Crockett of the State of Tennessee for revealing the "backwoods Anglo-Irishman as an uncivilized animal."

In the ensuing twenty-seven years Crockett almost ceased to exist as a historical figure, only surviving in the realm of folklore beside such figures as Paul Bunyan, Johnny Appleseed, and Pecos Bill. However, in 1954 his resurrection arrived in the form of the Walt Disney television drama *Davy Crockett, King of the Wild Frontier,* an entertaining mix of fact and fiction. With Texan Fess Parker as the easy-going, affable Tennessean, and a catchy theme song, the three-part series was an instant success, dramatizing the frontiersman's experiences in the Creek War, in Congress, and at the Alamo, bringing his name and legend to the attention of every adult and child in the United States, and launching an unprecedented merchandising campaign. One hundred and nineteen years after his death he once again took his place among the most celebrated and beloved men in American history. Even so, John Fischer, Rhodes scholar and editor of *Harper's* magazine, among a handful of others, was unimpressed and decided to enlighten the country about the man as Parrington had thirty years earlier. In a July 1955 column, Fischer identified Crockett as little more than a youthful juvenile delinquent and an "indolent and shiftless" adult. His attack did not strike at Crockett exclusively, since Fischer wrote that the citizens of his home state of Texas were brainwashed and deluded about the Alamo in general. The Tennessean survived this attack in no small part due to the Disney film, which inspired a loyal cadre of baby boomers destined to become the Alamo historians and biographers of the future.

In 1975, serious questions were raised about Crockett's death with the publication of *With Santa Anna in Texas: A Personal Narrative of the Revolution by José Enrique de la Peña,* translated and edited by Texas archivist Carmen Perry. Marketed as the campaign "diary" by the aide to Colonel Francisco Duque, leader of an attack column during the Alamo battle, the book received praise as a long-awaited and much-needed eyewitness chronicle of the Texas revolution from a Mexican perspective. *With Santa Anna in Texas* contained one paragraph mentioning the execution of Texan prisoners following the fall of the Alamo. In this version, as in the one related by Santa Anna's secretary, Ramón Martínez Caro, General Castrillón, who had taken over Duque's column during the attack, brought the Texans before Santa Anna. However, in the De la Peña account there were not five prisoners, as reported by Caro and Susannah Dickinson, but seven, reflecting the early stories of the executions originating in Sam Houston's correspondence. It identified one of the prisoners as "naturalist David Crocket, very well known in North America for his strange adventures, who had come to travel over the country and had been in Bejar [San Antonio] in the moment of surprise [and] had locked himself up in the Alamo, fearful that his quality as a foreigner would not be respected." The account described Crockett as "one of great stature, well formed and of regular features in whose countenance there was imprinted the sentiment of adversity, but in which was noted a certain resignation and nobility that commended him." In the De la Peña version, Santa Anna did not reprimand Castrillón as Caro had described, but merely denied the prisoners mercy with a gesture of indignation. When soldiers who were ordered to shoot the defenders hesitated, certain Mexican officers standing nearby jumped forward with swords to torment and kill the prisoners. The purported diary stated that the Americans "died moaning, but without humiliating themselves to their executioners."

Although the De la Peña document had been published in Spanish twenty years earlier in Mexico, and had been cited in a number of works in the United States, historians and the media reacted as if it had been newly discovered and doted on the irony of Crockett as executed prisoner in contrast to the cherished stories of his death, such as those drawn from the Disney or John Wayne films.

Revisionist historians in the cynical environment of the Vietnam and Watergate era found the "new" material irresistible, but in the rush to accept the De la Peña story no one bothered to establish whether the handwritten pages, upon which the book was based, were, in fact, authentic. Then, twenty years after its publication, a study of the manuscript revealed that it was actually comprised of a number of different documents, only one of which appeared to have been written by De la Peña—and it a mundane record of his activities on the Texan campaign. These pages contained one line describing the Alamo—"On the 6th the attack on the fortress of the Alamo was made the details of which are described separately"—making no mention of Crockett or of executions after the battle. Further investigation revealed that the papers serving as the principal source of the published book contained serious anomalies: not one page of it was written in De la Peña's hand, there was evidence of its having been compiled from historical sources made public after De la Peña's death, and there was a troubling lack of provenance—all indicators of a historical forgery.

Recently, forensic tests on the document, conducted by

graduate students of the University of Texas at Austin, revealed that the paper of the single page containing the information on Crockett is a common type, described as "laid" paper, and that it could not be matched to the type of paper of any other pages in its particular stack. Seventy-nine of the eighty-two sheets of paper in this stack measured twelve and a quarter by eight and a half inches and were folded in half, making a "quarto" of four writing surfaces. The page containing the description of Crockett's execution was only one of three single sheets of paper, six and an eighth by eight and a half inches, giving it the appearance of having been added as an afterthought. This was information that professors and officials from the university, writing articles and delivering talks on the authenticity of the De la Peña papers, have scrupulously avoided making public.

While the debate continues over its authenticity, the holograph De la Peña manuscript is housed at the Center for American History at the University of Texas at Austin, where it is treated as a near-holy relic. Historians, however, no longer regard it as a "diary," preferring to call it a research "memoir," and have ceased to accept it as a reliable source on the Texas revolution, the Alamo, or Crockett's death.

Although the dubious De la Peña account describes Crockett meeting his death with dignity and says nothing about him behaving dishonorably, it marked the beginning of the final sundering of his reputation. After its publication, articles began to appear under titles such as: "Did Davy Crockett Die at the Alamo?" "Crockett's Death at the Alamo Doubted," and "Davy Crockett—He Was Hardly King of the Wild Frontier."

Archivist Carmen Perry suffered abuse and harassment for the publication of *With Santa Anna* despite the fact that she had only translated the De la Peña document from Spanish to English. Dan Kilgore, a friend of Perry's and president of the Texas State Historical Association, came to her defense three years later with the publication of a slim volume *How Did Davy Die?* in which he demonstrated that the alleged De la Peña document was not the first to suggest Crockett had been executed, and that his execution, if it did occur, did nothing to diminish Crockett's heroism. The book, as before, generated newspaper stories ridiculing the hero and the public's admiration of him—"David Crockett Not the Idol You Think, Debunkers Say," "Ol' Davy Was No Big Deal," "Hero or Hoax," and "Davy Crockett Was No Great Shakes, the Debunkers Say."

Once the story of Crockett's execution became accepted, many historians and journalists were able to make the inductive leap to conclude that he surrendered at the Alamo, including in this conclusion the sop that no fault should be found in an honorable surrender in the face of overwhelming odds. Once the Mexican army had taken possession of the Alamo's walls, surrender would have been the logical path for the defenders if there were any hope of mercy, these stories suggested. However, in the Alamo context, the word "surrender" is virtually sacrilegious since the enduring legacy of the battle involves all of its men willingly fighting to the death, and that, in any event, Santa Anna's red flag of "no quarter" precluded the possibility of mercy. While historians explained that Crockett did nothing wrong in surrendering, some suggest that he may have done a little "fast talking" at the end to try to save his skin. The implication is that he, as the greatest symbolic leader of the Alamo defense, encouraged all the others to fight to the death but when his time came he decided that it was not such a good idea after all. The fact that Carmen Perry herself pointed out that the word "surrender," or even "capture," is never used in the De la Peña account made no impression on those determined to revise a historical record that probably required no revision.

In 1990, a writer named Jeff Long picked up the surrender story and took it to its ultimate level of ridicule in his book, *Duel of Eagles*, in which he typified Texas revolutionaries as bearing the "stink of ignorant, trigger-pulling white trash," with dirt under their fingernails and lice in their hair. He wrote, "David Crockett made a choice. The Go Ahead man quit. He did more than quit. He lied. He denied his role in the fighting."

In 1994, in Mark Derr's biography, *The Frontiersman: The Real Life and Many Legends of Davy Crockett*, the author wrote, "A number of historians have decided he hid under a bed during the final assault on the Alamo, was captured, and then killed after trying to lie his way out of difficulty by claiming he was there by accident," citing no works nor naming any historians as the source of this information. He then stated, quite correctly, "A review of the record proves these to be convenient fictions that are more revealing of their authors' ideologies and the times in which they have worked than of Crockett." Still, the author barely controlled his disdain for his subject as he described the Tennessean as a drunk, brawler, womanizer, adulterer, upstart, liar, loser, and hypocrite.

Finally, Alex Shoumatoff, in his 1997 *Legends of the American Desert: Sojourns in the Greater Southwest*, concluded the efforts to assassinate Crockett's memory and reputation when he declared, "Davy Crockett never wore a coonskin cap and, according to recent research, hid under a bed throughout the fighting [at the Alamo] and tried to surrender rather than fight to the death." As with Derr's work, Shoumatoff did not identify whose "recent research" provided this remarkable information. Based on Shoumatoff's one sentence on Crockett, unsupported by any documentation or footnotes, one review of his book was entitled "Davy Crockett Was a Coward."

The Symbol

I n July 1940, in an article in the *Southwest Review*, historian Walter Blair identified six distinct David Crocketts: the historical man, the Jacksonian hero, the Jacksonian villain, the Whig hero, the Whig villain (these four dependent on whether he was pro- or anti-Jackson at the time), and the fantastic character of the almanacs. One could add to this list the exploitable Crockett, as used by fly-by-night authors and land speculators for personal gain.

There is also the mythical, symbolic Crockett. Paintings and illustrations of the battle of the Alamo often show him as the central figure, using his rifle as a club against the horde of Mexican soldiers before being overwhelmed. The most famous of these images is Robert Jenkins Onderdonk's 1903 "Fall of the Alamo" painting, in which Crockett is shown just inside the south wall of the Alamo with a small group of his followers, meeting the advance of Mexican soldiers who have just charged through the gate. The Tennessean holds his rifle high over his head with his chest thrust forward, ready to accept the swords and bayonets of the enemy. This artwork, as with many other examples, is not documented history but a symbolic representation of the Alamo story in general—a small, resolute band fighting to the death against great odds. Crockett, as the best known defender of the Alamo, was the logical choice for this representation.

Walt Disney's famed production reinforced this symbolic image in 1955 with its last episode, "Davy Crockett at the Alamo." In the final moments of the battle, Crockett's close companions are picked off one by one, leaving him as the last surviving Alamo defender. With bullets whizzing by him he takes his position at the top of a stairway to a parapet on the Alamo's wall. As Mexican soldiers charge up the stairway toward him, he flails away at them with his rifle. We never see what happens to him since the scene fades to the Alamo's flag, and then to the modern Lone Star flag of Texas, but the implication is that he went down fighting. If not completely factual, it was an exciting, climatic scene—symbolic of the stand at the Alamo.

In 1960, John Wayne, America's favorite actor, portrayed Crockett in *The Alamo*, a film that he also produced and directed. Larger-than-life himself, Wayne played the Tennessean accordingly, depicting him as a somewhat self-conscious celebrity, but fully aware of his status and how to influence people with it. His group of Tennesseans follow him to Texas to hunt, drink, and have a good time, but he leads them there intending to join the revolution already in progress. Once in San Antonio he describes to them what is at stake in Texas's bid for freedom by falsifying a letter from Santa Anna threatening to "chastise them even unto death," if they do not leave the territory. One of his men protests getting mixed up in someone else's revolution, stating that it is not their "ox that's a-getting gored." By the time Crockett gets around to telling them that he had written the letter, the men have already worked themselves into a fever pitch against Santa Anna and unanimously decide to fight against him.

Wayne's version of Davy's death scene has Mexican soldiers surging over the Texans' last, hastily constructed redoubt in front of the Alamo church while Crockett, with rifle in one hand and a flaming torch in the other, runs toward the church. He stops and turns outside the church doors, throwing his rifle at two Mexican soldiers and hitting another one with the torch. He is immediately impaled, pinned to the door by a lance, breaks the shaft with a flick of his wrist, staggers into the church, and dies in the act of blowing up the Alamo's gunpowder supply. As in the case of the Disney film there is more drama and symbolism than history in Wayne's *The Alamo*.

Since 1910, Crockett has been portrayed no less than thirty times in films, both silent and sound. In 2004, Touchstone Pictures resurrected his memory, as its parent company, Walt Disney Studios, had fifty years earlier, with its new production of *The Alamo*. This time screenwriters sought both to tell the story of the Alamo and establish the character of Crockett more realistically. Character actor Billy Bob Thornton portrayed the Tennessean as a good-humored, almost apologetic former congressman who reacts with some dismay upon reaching San Antonio and finding that the fighting is not over.

Thornton's Crockett is a fiddle player who totes his instrument all the way from Tennessee to the Alamo, and in one of the more interesting scenes in the film, while the Mexican army's band performs the "Deguello," a musical piece adapted from their bugle call promising "no quarter," Crockett mounts the wall of the Alamo and accompanies the band on his fiddle. The haunting piece, written by composer Carter Burwell, lulls both Texan and Mexican combatants into a moment of peaceful reflection. On the surface, Crockett answers Santa Anna's musical announcement of no mercy with one of his own, impressing upon the Mexican soldiers that they will have no easy time of it and that the Texans will fight. Below the surface the scene serves as an antiwar message, showing through the commonality of the music that the opposing forces have few differences.

In recent years some historians have tried to minimize the image of an aggressive Crockett in presenting their spin on the details of his service in the Texas revolution. If he had been a jingoistic troublemaker, spoiling for a fight, then a reasonable conclusion could be drawn that he got what he deserved at the Alamo. If he had been a reluctant warrior, then his death in the battle is all the more poignant. These historians have taken the curious slant of portraying him as traveling to San Antonio only because he was "embarrassed" into doing so, then, when he could not extricate himself from service graciously, becoming trapped by his own legend. While there is no historical evidence for this, the idea was depicted in the new film when Thornton's Crockett expresses this sentiment to Jim Bowie.

The makers of the film were faced with the problem of presenting Crockett's death in a way that brought something new to the mix, so as not to appear repetitive of earlier efforts. They did this by toning down any suggestions of an overly glorious or mythically heroic death to bring the character of Crockett to a more human level. Some attention also may have been paid to the fear that the legendary American courageously bashing away at Mexican soldiers would offend or alienate certain segments of a multicultural audience.

In the final moments of the cinematic battle, Crockett and his men group together inside the Alamo church waiting for the Mexican soldiers to break through the doors. Crockett has time to exchange a glance with a small Tejano boy, peeking out of a room where the women and children are sheltered. His expression indicates that he will not let the boy down in his last stand, but it also indicates that he will not fail in what is expected of him in living up to his legend. The Mexican troops finally break through, charge in, and join battle with this last knot of defenders.

The action then stops and in the next scene Crockett kneels before Santa Anna in front of the Alamo church, his hands tied behind his back. Of all the Texans making their last stand together, he is the only one who has survived the final onslaught, with the circumstances of how he alone came to be taken prisoner never explained. Bloodied but unbowed, Crockett's demeanor is not one of supplication. He defiantly taunts Santa Anna with a bit of grim humor, remarking that he thought the general would have been taller. He also offers Santa Anna and his army the opportunity to lay down their arms and surrender to *him*, promising that he will intercede with Sam Houston for mercy on their behalf. This is all that the Mexican dictator will stand, and he orders his execution. A group of Mexican soldiers, standing nearby, descend on Crockett and slash him to death with bayonets.

Thornton's Crockett is no more or less heroic than in earlier films, nor is his character any more historically accurate than previous onscreen portrayals—it is just inaccurate in different ways. However, Thorton's performance does give the character new dimension and undeniable appeal. Not surprisingly, Crockett emerges as the most interesting figure in the production and may well inspire another generation to seek out the man behind the movies and the myths.

David Crockett came to national prominence at a time when the Founding Fathers were passing from the scene and the American identity was shifting from the Virginia aristocracy to the common man of the Western frontier.

While the Tennessean did not become a great explorer in the tradition of Lewis and Clark, or a colonizer like Daniel Boone, he did contribute to the development of Tennessee in a steadfast, if not a flamboyant, way. In his lifelong journey westward in the state, he helped establish settlements, enforce laws, and develop roads. As a legislator he fought ceaselessly for the interests of his people and served as an exemplar of the American ideal of an ordinary man rising above his station to a position of national eminence. As a military man he wore no medals or fancy uniform, but served as a volunteer in Andrew Jackson's bloody Indian battles in Alabama, and as a scout and hunter.

In leaving the United States and traveling to Mexican Texas in 1836, he hoped to start a new life for himself and his family. In the Texas revolution he paid the ultimate price and did, in fact, provide a home for his family as his wife, Elizabeth, son

Robert, and his younger children later moved to Texas on land entitled to him for his service in the revolution.

The 2004 Alamo film may renew interest in the historical David Crockett. If the past is any indication, some are sure to follow the Crockett trail from one film to the next, searching for a portrayal of the man that most satisfies their expectations of him, and may continue on, wading across rivers of myths, legends, and fiction of the ring-tailed roarer, the uncouth frontier buffoon, and the phony coward. If they find their way through the dense forests and misleading paths of revisionist history, the persistent searchers will have the privilege of meeting the Honorable David Crockett, husband, father, farmer, hunter, soldier, legislator, United States congressman, author, and genuine American hero.

ACKNOWLEDGMENTS AND SOURCES

Thanks to my wife, Kelly, daughter, Katie, and our Weimaraner, Brooklyn Dodger, for their patience and support during the writing of this hook. Also thanks to Tom Doherty of Forge Books, and literary agent Nat Sobel, for giving me this opportunity; and especially to editor Dale L. Walker, who expended gallons of green ink in guiding me through this process. I am most grateful to fellow members of the Western Writers of America—Lori Van Pelt, Candy Moulton, and Jim Crutchfield—all writing books in the American Heroes series, for their suggestions, guidance, and occasional pep talks.

Among the community of Crockett and Alamo historians and enthusiasts I received a great deal of help and material from such friends as William R. Chemerka, Paul Andrew Hutton, Brian Huberman, Michael A. Lofaro, William C. Davis, and especially Thomas Ricks Lindley.

Elaine B. Davis and her staff at the Daughters of the Republic of Texas Library at the Alamo were very helpful, as always, as was the staff at the Butt-Holdsworth Memorial Library in Kerr-ville, Texas.

I thank my friends Joe Musso, Jeff Beardon, and Bill Gatlin, who keep the memory of heroes such as David Crockett and Jim Bowie alive, and who were always willing to share some observations with me.

Thanks to my friend, former classmate, and kid from the old neighborhood, Connie Boylan, for her help with information on music and for her interest in seeing this project completed.

Indispensable for a study of David Crockett are the words of Crockett himself in *An Account of Col. Crockett's Tour to the North and Down East* (Philadelphia: E. L. Carey and A. Hart, 1835; reprint, New York: Nafis & Cornish, 1845), and *A Narrative of the Life of David Crockett* (Philadelphia: E. L. Carey and A. Hart, 1834; reprint, Lincoln: University of Nebraska Press, 1987, with an introduction by Paul Andrew Hutton). While scholars generally agree that the *Tour to the North and Down East* was ghostwritten, it was done so with Crockett's assistance and remembrances of his trip.

Paul Hutton writes of Crockett as he would an old friend. Besides his introduction to *A Narrative of the Life*, I highly recommend his articles, "Davy Crockett, Still King of the Wild Frontier" (*Texas Monthly*, November 1986); "'Going to Congress and making allmynacks is my trade.' Davy Crockett, His Almanacs, and the Evolution of a Frontier Legend" (*Journal of the West*, April 1998); "Mr. Crockett Goes to Washington" (*American History*, April 2000); "On the Crockett Trail" (*Roundup Magazine*, December 2002); and "Davy Crockett's Bloody Vest" (*Roundup Magazine*, August 2003).

James Atkins Shackford's *David Crockett: The Man and the*

Legend (Chapel Hill: University of North Carolina Press, 1956) is a landmark book and the first attempting to retrieve Crockett's memory from the realm of folklore.

Several other works are important for separating David Crockett the man from the legend. These are: Richard Boyd Hauck's *Crockett: A Bio-Bibliography* (Westport, CT: Greenwood Press, 1982); Michael A. Lofaro and Joe Cummings, editors, *Crockett at Two-Hundred: New Perspectives on the Man and the Myth* (Knoxville, TN: University of Tennessee Press, 1989); and Michael A. Lofaro, editor, *Davy Crockett: The Man, the Legend, the Legacy 1786–1986* (Knoxville, TN: University of Tennessee Press, 1985).

William R. Chemerka's *The Davy Crockett Almanac and Book of Lists* (Austin, TX: Eakin Press, 2000) is an encyclopedia-like guide to the Crockett of history and popular culture. It is a handy and entertaining reference. Chemerka also has published the *Alamo Journal* for twenty years, and more recently the *Crockett Chronicle,* both valuable sources for information on the Tennessean of fact and fiction.

William C. Davis's *Three Roads to the Alamo: The Lives and Fortunes of David Crockett, James Bowie, and William Barret Travis* (New York: HarperCollins, 1998) traces the paths of Crockett, Bowie, and Travis from birth to their deaths at the Alamo. His Crockett material, a book within a book, brings a fresh perspective to the story and corrects some long-standing misinterpretations that date back to Shackford's original study.

Mark Derr, *The Frontiersman: The Real Life and the Many Legends of Davy Crockett* (New York: William Morrow, 1993), is a well-researched and detailed biography, but to the author's obvious dislike of his subject is added his almost blue-nosed obsession with the Tennessean as a "drunk," and anything else to do with drinks, drinking, and alcohol in general.

Gary L. Foreman's well-illustrated *Crockett: The Gentleman from the Cane* (Dallas, TX: Taylor Publishing Co., 1986) is a great visual connection to the people, places, and things in Crockett's life. It also brings together in one volume six of the congressman's portraits done from life.

Joseph John Arpad's doctoral dissertation, *David Crockett, An Original Eccentricity and Early American Character* (Department of English, Duke University, December 21, 1969), is important in showing Crockett's development in conjunction with that of the stage character Nimrod Wildfire.

Curtis Carroll Davis's "A Legend at Full-Length. Mr. Chapman Paints Colonel Crockett—and Tells About It" (Proceedings of the American Antiquarian Society, 1960) and Frederick S. Voss's "Portraying an American Original: The Likenesses of Davy Crockett" (*Southwestern Historical Quarterly*, April 1988) tell the story of Crockett's artistic representations in relation to the subject's growing awareness of his own public image.

John Seelye's introduction and annotations to Richard Penn Smith's *On to the Alamo: Colonel Crockett's Exploits and Adventures in Texas* (New York: Penguin Classics, 2003) clear up the confusion regarding this fictional work that has influenced so many later histories.

Manley F. Cobia's *Journey into the Land of Trials: The Story of Davy Crockett's Expedition to the Alamo* (Franklin, TN: Hillsboro Press, 2003) is a well-researched and well-written account of Crockett's final journey from Tennessee to Texas and the Alamo.

Thomas Ricks Lindley's *Alamo Traces: New Evidence and*

New Conclusions (Lanham, MD: Republic of Texas Press, 2003) is simply the most important book on the Alamo to appear in years. Lindley's meticulous research has added a new dimension to Crockett's last heroic acts at the Alamo.

Regarding eyewitness accounts of the battle of the Alamo, and the ongoing controversy about Crockett's death, I referred to material previously published in my own books: In *Death of a Legend: The Myth and Mystery Surrounding the Death of Davy Crockett* (Plano, TX: Republic of Texas Press, 1999) I explain the legend of Crockett being among those executed after the Alamo battle. In *Eyewitness to the Alamo* (revised edition, Plano, TX: Republic of Texas Press, 2001), I present over one hundred eyewitness or alleged eyewitness accounts of the siege and battle, most of which form the basis for our knowledge of what happened at the Alamo.

OTHER BOOKS AND ARTICLES CONSULTED

Aderman, Ralph M., editor. *The Letters of James Kirke Paulding.* Madison, WI: University of Wisconsin Press, 1962.

Baldwin, Christopher Columbus. *Diary of Christopher Columbus Baldwin, Librarian of the American Antiquarian Society.* Worcester, MA.: American Antiquarian Society, 1901.

Bass, Feris A., and B. R. Brunson, editors. *Fragile Empires: The Texas Correspondence of Samuel Swartwout and James Morgan.* Austin: Shoal Creek Publishers, 1978.

Blair, Walter, "Six Davy Crocketts . . ." *Southwest Review,* 1940.

Chemerka, William R., "Davy Crockett's New Jersey Tour," *New Jersey Heritage Magazine,* 2001.

Crutchfield, James A. *Davy Crockett's Almanacks 1835–1843. The Nashville Imprints.* Union City, TN: Pioneer Press, 1986.

Davis, James D. *The History of the City of Memphis.* Memphis, TN: Hite, Crumpton & Kelly, Printers, 1873.

Derby, J. C. *Fifty Years Among Authors, Books and Publishers.* Chicago: People's Publishing Company, 1884.

Harrison, Lowell H., "David Crockett," *American History Illustrated,* July 1971.

Heale, M. J., "The Role of the Frontier in Jacksonian Politics: David Crockett and the Myth of the Self-Made Man," *Western Historical Quarterly,* October 1973.

Kelly, James C. and Frederick S. Voss. *Davy Crockett: Gentleman from the Cane.* Washington, D.C., and Nashville, TN: National Portrait Gallery and the Tennessee State Museum, 1986.

Kilgore, Dan. *How Did Davy Die?* College Station: Texas A&M University Press, 1978.

Lalire, Gregory J., "David Crockett," *American History,* February 2004.

Long, Jeff. *Duel of Eagles: The Mexican and U.S. Fight for the Alamo.* New York: William Morrow, 1990.

Lord, Walter. *A Time to Stand.* New York: Harper & Row, 1961.

Miles, Guy S., "David Crockett Evolves, 1821–1824," *American Quarterly,* 1956.

Palmquist, Robert F., "High Private: David Crockett at the Alamo," *Real West,* December 1981.

———, "Mr. Crockett Goes to Washington," *Real West,* October 1981.

Parrington, Vernon Louis. *The Romantic Revolution in America 1800–1860.* New York: Harcourt Brace Jovanovich, 1927; reprint, Norman, OK: University of Oklahoma Press, 1987.

Perry, Carmen, trans. and ed. *With Santa Anna in Texas: A Personal Narrative of the Revolution by José Enrique de la Peña.* College Station: Texas A&M University Press, 1975.

Shoumatoff, Alex. *Legends of the American Desert: Sojourns in the Greater Southwest.* New York: Alfred A. Knopf, 1997.

Smith, Jonathan Kennon Thompson. *The Land Holdings of Colonel David Crockett in West Tennessee.* Jackson, TN: privately published, December 2003.

Stout, S. H., "David Crockett," *American Historical Magazine,* January 1902.

Swisher, John M. *The Swisher Memoirs.* Edited by Rena Maverick Green. San Antonio: n.p., 1932.

Timanus, Rod. *On the Crockett Trail.* Union City, TN: Pioneer Press, 1999.

Wade, J. D., "The Authorship of David Crockett's 'Autobiography,'" *The Georgia Historical Quarterly,* September 1922.

William Groneman III is recently retired from the
New York City Fire Department with the rank of
captain after a twenty-four-year career. At the
time of his retirement, he was the company
commander of Engine Company 308 and worked at
Ground Zero just hours after the attack on the
World Trade Center on September 11, 2001.
A longtime student of Texas history, in particular
the Texas republic era, he has written several books
and many articles exploring the myths and
misconceptions surrounding the
Battle of the Alamo.